Fail-Safe Small Businesses

Fail-Safe Small Businesses

How They Work,
Why They Succeed

Ron Tepper

JOHN WILEY & SONS, INC.
New York • Chichester • Brisbane • Toronto • Singapore

This publication is designed to provide accurate and authoritative
information in regard to the subject matter covered. It is sold with the
understanding that the publisher is not engaged in rendering legal,
accounting, or other professional services. If legal advice or other
expert assistance is required, the services of a competent professional
person should be sought.

Library of Congress Cataloging-in-Publication Data

Tepper, Ron, 1937–
    Fail-safe small businesses: how they work, why they succeed / by
Ron Tepper.
       p. cm.
    Includes bibliographical references.
    ISBN 0-471-01438-9. — ISBN 0-471-01437-0 (pbk.)
    1. Small business—United States—Management—Case studies.
2. Success in business—United States—Case studies. I. Title.
HD62.7.T46 1994
658.02'2—dc20   93-34132
                                          CIP

Printed in the United States of America
10 9 8 7 6 5 4 3 2 1

Contents

CONTENTS

Introduction

While many large corporations are running into difficulties, downsizing, outsourcing, losing their best employees as well as millions of dollars, thousands of small businesses in this country are growing and prospering.

All of these enterprises operate in the same economic environment as IBM and General Motors, yet they are run so well that they have become virtually "failure-proof."

What is there about these businesses that differentiates them from enterprises that are barely surviving? How did they start, where did the capital come from, how are they managed, what do they do to market their products and services, and why are they so profitable?

To find the answers to those questions, more than a dozen highly profitable, small business enterprises were closely examined and their owners were interviewed for this book. The businesses cover a broad gamut, from consulting and janitorial services, to dog grooming and publishing representatives. The businesses are in categories ranging from retail to service; the owners range from college graduates to high school dropouts.

Among their number are: Jay Horoki, an accounting

major who was less than a year away from entering a profitable profession. Yet he gave it all up to open a janitorial service, where he earned more than $100,000 his first year. Lana McKendry is a former waitress who sat down to evaluate "where she was going" and decided she needed a direction. She found one, and her young manufacturer's rep company earned more than $20 million in revenue in its seventh year of operation.

Jerry Turner, a New Mexico native, "always wanted to be his own boss." Now he is, and this year his striping/paving company will generate more than $2 million. Mike Goldberg is a New Yorker who developed a new approach to dealing with magazine publishers and their advertisers; this technique will earn him more than $150,000 this year.

Kendall Shurcut, a young, ambitious West Coast native, turned his fondness for animals into a professional grooming business that has given him freedom and an income that places him in the top 10 percent of all wage earners. Bob Levinson, a frustrated Madison Avenue advertising executive, got out of agency business, developed an unusual "menu" approach to advertising services, and today works with nearly 40 small business clients.

And there are more: Tony Walton is a computer consultant; Dennis McCuistion is a banking consultant; Ginny Anderson is a mobile dog groomer; Vicky Harrington is the owner of a valet parking service; Delia Ornaz is a young woman who built an enormously successful maid service business.

They are a diverse group who have many characteristics in common. Each person had extensive experience in the business before striking out on his or her own. Nearly all of their businesses had low start-up costs (most were launched for under $10,000) and low overhead. None spend abnormal sums on marketing or advertising, but they all have developed unique, low-cost techniques to reach their customers and expand their market share.

Some of these businesses are in small market areas, while others are located in large, metropolitan centers. Every one of them, however, can be taken and placed almost anywhere in the country, as long as the owner's operating techniques are followed.

The principles these entrepreneurs utilized in order to become a success are equally as important as the type of businesses. These techniques apply not only to the fail-safe enterprises in this book, but to every business.

An important point that every one of these entrepreneurs makes is that you do not have to duplicate the business they created in order to be successful—only their techniques.

In addition, aside from interviews with the entrepreneurs who created these fail-safe businesses, readers will also find advice and comments from some of the most successful small businesspeople in the country—individuals who validate the approach that each of the fail-safe owners has taken.

Fail-Safe Small Businesses is about more than a group of enterprises that have managed to prosper despite difficult economic times. It is about a group of entrepreneurs, each taking a different path, but who all ultimately succeeded because they adhered to sound business principles.

Even more, it is about people and the successful small businesses they created—businesses that have not only proven to be viable today but can be duplicated by other ambitious entrepreneurs tomorrow.

Fail-Safe Small Businesses

1

Why Businesses Fail

There are few places more difficult to launch a business than New York City. But for Mike Goldberg, it was "easier than I thought." Goldberg, who started his enterprise when most businesses were downsizing or going through extreme financial hardships, will earn more than $150,000 this year—and he opened his doors less than two years ago with an investment of just over $1,000. The same enterprise could be started today, with the exact same investment, and it could be equally as successful.

Three thousand miles away, Joel Kirk is going through an experience exactly the opposite of Mike's. Instead of euphoria, he is feeling depressed. And no wonder. He lost not only his business but his home and life savings as well. Kirk invested more than $500,000 in a venture that he thought could not lose. It did.

In Chicago, Lillian Helmers sits inside her Michigan Avenue art supply store and wonders why there is no business. She watches her two clerks, both art students, shuffle back and forth between aisles, straightening supplies and waiting for customers. Her capital is rapidly disappearing, and her outlook is similar to Kirk's.

What is the difference among Goldberg, Kirk, and Helmers? Why did one hit it big with a relatively insignificant investment, while the other two failed with an enormous capital expenditure?

Goldberg became a publishing representative, Kirk opened a restaurant, and, of course, Helmers ran an art supply store. One significant difference is in their business backgrounds. Kirk knew little about restaurants, and Helmers knew even less about art supply stores. Goldberg, however, had 15 years of publishing experience before he opened his rep firm.

THE IMPORTANCE OF INDUSTRY EXPERIENCE

Experience is critical to small business success. Experience means knowledge of the industry, competitors and customers. One major common characteristic that every "failure-proof" entrepreneur in this book has is *background*. All knew their industry or business before they invested in it. Small business people take risks, but successful ones do not fly blind.

Retail businesses and those dependent on consumer whims are replete with pitfalls. Restaurants top the list of enterprises that fail most often. Yet budding entrepreneurs often opt to own their own eateries. For example, like Joel Kirk, Ralph Menlo dreamed of his own restaurant for years. He was a successful magazine editor and writer, and says, "I can just see myself welcoming people at the door and presiding over a packed house every night."

Fortunately, Menlo never invested any of his hard-earned writing revenue in roasts or ribs. But he does provide a clue as to why so many want to enter the field.

"Everyone in America eats, so why wouldn't a restaurant be a success? It seems to me—and many others— a glamorous field as well. Imagine being just inside the door, alongside the maitre d', and welcoming people as they come flocking into your restaurant. You're a minicelebrity. It conjures up images of old, great movies like *Casablanca*, where Rick [Humphrey Bogart] owned his own club. There's something enormously appealing about it."

Glamour, being your own boss and "calling the shots," are definitely appealing. But it is not easy. Menlo and other budding restaurant owners seldom think about food spoilage, labor problems, consistency of meals, location, lack of buying skills, marketing and promotional dollars required, undercapitalization, and, of course, the economy. Those pitfalls haunt every business that has perishable products and depends on consumers.

Joel Kirk's lack of expertise in the field did not help, but the economy's nosedive proved to be the death knell for his exclusive dinner house.

Tough times have an impact not only on mid- and high-priced dinner houses, they also alter the habits of families that eat at relatively inexpensive fast-food restaurants. During the past few years, such places as McDonald's, Burger King, and Taco Bell have introduced a great many "low-priced" dinner menus. The food industry recognizes the consumer's belt-tightening, and if restaurant owners want to stay in business, they have to listen to their customers. Even then they may not be able to survive.

THE IMPACT OF A RECESSION

Joel Kirk opened the wrong business at the wrong time. He served his first meal and patron in May 1991, the country was in a recession. Giving up a night on the town is relatively easy, especially if you are without a job or your position is tenuous. National unemployment and downsizing continue.

The recent recession hit mid- and upper-priced restaurants particularly hard. Unlike previous economic downturns, which primarily impacted blue-collar workers, this recession, which has plagued the country since the late 1980s, has been a disaster for white-collar workers. And white-collar workers are the prime customers of upscale restaurants.

Recessions and/or tough times impact other small businesses as well. Take, for instance, the furniture and/or appliance store or the new car dealer. These enterprises suffer because consumers are not interested in buying durable goods when the future is uncertain. Over the past two to three years furniture retailer ranks have been decimated, as have been automobile dealerships. Entrepreneurs dreaming of opening durable goods outlets should think twice. In today's economy, most of those businesses are headed for failure.

The changing lifestyle of Americans is accelerating the problem of trying to open and run a viable durable goods business. Their tastes are going from BMWs to econovans and Jeeps, a phenomenon that is explored in Chapter 5.

In tough times, consumers traditionally repair and renovate. New home sales and resales of properties slow down. People tighten their belts and wait. While the real estate industry suffers, home remodeling/repair and swap meets where merchandise can be bought at a discount boom. People stay where they are. They even cut their vacations from two weeks in Europe to five days at Yosemite.

Businesspeople who ignore these trends risk disaster. Failure rates for repair/renovation enterprises are insignificant, and most have an excellent chance of becoming profitable with low start-up investments.

THE FIVE CAUSES OF SMALL BUSINESS FAILURE

If we examine the economy and the entrepreneurs who try to defy the odds, the causes for small business failures are no mystery. For the most part, they are the result of the entrepreneur failing to examine the five key elements:

poor business choice
poor location

poor employees

poor management

poor marketing strategy

Poor Business Choice

Kirk's high-priced restaurant opened in the midst of a recession, and illustrates poor business choice. A similar poor business choice might be opening a Mexican restaurant next door to a senior citizens' complex. Senior citizens tend to shy away from spicy, hot foods.

By "poor business choices" I mean enterprises that do not meet the needs of prospective customers. Consider, for example, an animal grooming parlor in a low-income neighborhood or located near an apartment complex where animals are prohibited; an advertising and public relations consulting agency in a community without businesses; or a janitorial service in an area without commercial properties. Each situation displays the inability of the businessperson to empathize with customers and to understand where customers are, where they come from, and what they want. Successful entrepreneurs can put themselves in their customers' place and objectively ask "Would I buy this service or product?"

THE "CAN'T-MISS" PRODUCT

Some entrepreneurs believe their product or idea cannot miss because "everyone needs it," and they only need "a small portion of the market" to succeed. "There are more than 250 million people in this country, and less than 1 percent will make me a success," they tell themselves. Securing 1 percent of the market is easier said than done.

Competition prevents many entrepreneurs from making a go of a business. Just look at any supermarket, and consider the problems a manufacturer faces to get a product displayed, especially if it is the first product to be produced by a struggling young company.

Shelves are crowded, discounts are prevalent, name brands dominate, the store demands concessions, and advertising is expensive. Entrepreneurs find it difficult to supplant existing established products that sell, to convince a purchasing agent to take a new product.

Distributors are not interested in taking on a new product and fighting to win name recognition for it. They like the tried and true. Why not? Usually they make the same commission from either product. They have enough problems keeping their current line on the shelf. Why risk their position for a new product?

If a new product is the first (and only) one that a manufacturer offers, it is unlikely that a distributor will be interested unless the manufacturer's marketing strategy has already created a demand for the product. Simple Green, a cleaning product that has been around for about 15 years, is a classic example. The manufacturer tried for years to get it into stores. Occasionally he had minor successes with independent supermarkets. Most of the time, however, marketing efforts were frustrated due to the limited shelf space available for new products.

After nearly a dozen years of pushing the product, sales had slowly inched up into the seven-figure range. Still, the owner/manufacturer was earning little profit. Then one day a portion of the marketing strategy clicked. *Consumer Reports*, the national magazine that evaluates products, did extensive testing and a positive write-up on Simple Green. Within days stores were deluged with requests for the product, and 12 months later every major home center and supermarket chain was carrying it.

Poor Location

Have you chosen the right location? Poor location is a villain that is especially destructive when it comes to retail operations. With retail, the key to profitability is traffic. If a clothing, grocery, or furniture outlet is located off the beaten track, its survival and prosperity opportunities diminish. Sales predictions are off the mark if the business does not have easy access, or if it is located away from the areas where its customers can be found.

Let's consider local malls. Retailers pay premium rents and percentages because malls bring traffic. The major anchor tenants (department stores) advertise and drive customers through the mall. When a mall loses its anchor tenants, it is not long before many other retailers fail. Sometimes malls offer retailers inducements to locate in a center where there is no major anchor. Beware! That is no inducement at all. It's an invitation to failure.

Malls have personalities, too. Some are upscale, while others cater to the middle- and lower-income brackets. Several years ago a prominent California developer of malls eyed an exclusive high-income area of town and decided to build a mall there. His idea was to capture the discretionary dollars before they went anywhere else. He built the mall, lured several prominent anchors into the center, and opened. Unfortunately, because of the expensive location, the owner had to charge the retailers higher rents. In turn, the retailers passed those higher fees on to the customers. But the customers never arrived. They were knowledgeable about prices and recognized that this mall charged an average of 10 to 15 percent more for the same goods that could be purchased three miles away. Consumers, especially affluent ones, are not ignorant. Most did not get their money foolishly, and they know its value. They know other values, too. Consequently, they bypassed the mall and went to the friendly, lower-priced center to do their shopping. Today the mall stands half empty with little traffic, and the developer is burdened with a huge debt.

Even within a mall, shopping patterns and customers differ. The discount store at one end will draw one type clientele, while the department store at the other end will draw another. Shoppers do not necessarily traverse the entire mall. Some just come to buy at certain shops, and then they leave. Some come to the mall to window-shop; they never buy. Retailers who plan to locate in malls should study the crowd. Even a big one does not necessarily mean that buying is brisk. Are the people in the mall carrying packages? Did they buy? Or are they just spending an evening browsing through?

Consumers also are becoming aware that malls cost more. Most know that stores pay a premium to locate in malls and recognize that that premium is passed on to them in the form of higher prices. If you as a retailer are sold on a mall location, the first question to ask yourself is: Can I afford the rent and the percentage? Will I sell that many goods? Too many retailers forget to pose those questions. They sometimes forget that when consumer confidence lags, so does mall traffic and purchasing.

Service businesses seldom fail due to lack of traffic. Repair, maintenance, and consulting are not subject to impulse buying. Most service businesses can be located in low-rent strip centers, or even in commercial and industrial parks, because their patrons do not just happen to "walk in." In fact, in today's economy, in most areas of the country bargain office space is readily available to service entrepreneurs.

Service entrepreneurs don't need to rent high-priced space, and those who pay premium rents are usually spending capital needlessly. Still, some entrepreneurs are willing to pay more—for the prestige. Too many service business entrepreneurs still rent out of ego rather than need. A consultant has a choice in today's market—high overhead with an exclusive, prestigious office address; moderate overhead in a moderately priced office; or low overhead—at home. Many service business failures can be traced to unnecessary high-priced rentals.

Poor Employees

Employees can be an enormous problem, too. A poor receptionist can cost more business in a day than a firm can generate in a month. A discourteous service department can cause an equal amount of bad-mouthing by customers, and a poor service reputation spreads quickly. Small business lore is replete with stories of promising, profitable enterprises that went downhill because of the poor quality of the employees.

Poor selection of employees is also part of the reason for the downfall of one of the most successful small business manufacturers in the country. The company was Van Pler & Tissany, one of the most profitable firms to ever market high-grade cubic zirconians, or "CZs"—artificial diamonds.

Sales were skyrocketing, and the company was on the verge of opening satellite stores in affluent malls when things began to unravel. Customers became angry when they discovered their stones were not mounted correctly; customer service was rude, and orders arrived late. Bad word-of-mouth travels ten times faster than good. In Van Pler's case, it traveled at the speed of light.

The problem stemmed from rapid growth. The pressure on the manufacturing line was too much. As demand increased, workers could not produce the same quality goods. They took shortcuts to meet demand. Customers called to complain and ask for refunds, and the brusque, harried customer service personnel irritated clients.

Management was not totally unaware of what was happening. But the money kept rolling in, so executives chose to ignore the "minor" complaints. Business fell and before the owner could mend the fences, the firm's sales had been halved and its capital ran out. When the owners went to the bank for additional credit, the bankers drew back after scrutinizing the books and examining the sales trend.

In less than a year, the enterprise was gone. Once again, an employee problem was exacerbated by the failure of management to plan for growth and handle it.

Why are employees' job performances lacking? There are numerous reasons. Perhaps they have not "bought in" to the enterprise and view their job as just that, a job that will not last long. Not every firm can boast the loyalty and energy of a Federal Express or UPS. Both companies involve employees in the firm's overall goal, and employees are given an excellent chance to earn more when the company performs well. Employees who have a stake in the business do much better than those who do not.

In some cases, the entrepreneur who created the enterprise is at fault. He or she may have run the business alone for too long. When a business starts up, usually one or two employees, at most, are needed. In the early stages of development, many retail facilities hire just a few employees.

When a business is at that level, the founder can spend time watching, training, and being involved with employees. As the enterprise grows, however, the owner spends less time with existing employees and seldom screens new ones. The owner is too pressed to handle the traffic and get the goods out. Screening employees is down the priority list.

Poor Management

Some entrepreneurs do not know when to "let go," when to bring in a professional to manage the enterprise and handle employee problems. Small business owners frequently resist this step because it costs money, and the funds are not going directly to increase sales. The longer they insist on running the business and overseeing the employees, the organization has a greater chance for failure. The inability to recognize the need for professional human resource people can destroy a business—even a multimillion-dollar-a-year enterprise.

Take, for instance, *Entrepreneur* magazine. By 1981 it had grown to nearly $15 million a year in revenues. Four years earlier, its gross sales were in the area of $500,000. Yet despite the huge influx of capital, it was in Chapter 11 (bankruptcy) because management was not sophisticated enough to handle the rapid growth.

Most of the employees who were with the company initially advanced up the ladder as the company grew. Yet few were qualified to handle the rapid growth of a cash-intensive business. One executive, who had started in the mail room, eventually became president. Another found himself responsible for millions of dollars' worth of marketing expenditures.

Talented people can be found in the mail room, but in *Entrepreneur*'s case it did not happen. Although the company eventually emerged from bankruptcy, the media had a field day reporting on the "company that gave everyone advice on how to succeed in business forgot to heed its own."

Entrepreneur's painful predicament could have been avoided had the owner seen fit to bring a human resource department into the fold. A human resource department would have recognized how diversified the company had become and the new skills that were required.

Entrepreneur is not the only horror story. Tom Carns ran a $5 million-a-year company (PDQ Printing), and he was president of his national trade association. One month he was even on the cover of the industry's most prestigious magazine. His reputation was such that people around the country paid more than $3,000 apiece to spend a few days with him in his print shop and learn the ropes. His expertise was such that he began to do one-day seminars; he would leave his business for three days at a time, travel to a distant city, and teach other budding entrepreneurs how to run their businesses.

"I was so busy that I lost control," he says, "and one of my managers embezzled several thousand dollars." The business began to go downhill. Tom lost interest, and suddenly he found himself in bankruptcy court, trying to reorganize his company. Small businesses are not huge corporations, nor are they the government. They need constant stewardship. Forget that and the business can sink before anyone realizes it happened.

Ann Machado, founder and chief executive officer of Creative Staffing, a $12 million-a-year Miami-based temporary employment agency, recalls that she began making money in her second month of operation. Her business was so successful that everyone told her she should franchise the concept, and she did.

Her plan was to start a new company in another Florida city. Just before it was time to open, however, she was cautioned that this new city—Orlando—was different from Miami. She quickly discovered that the market was different, and so were her customers. The losses mounted. After watching $150,000 go through the door, she closed. The business may be proven and successful, but markets can differ. People differ.

Leif Blodee cofounded a furniture manufacturing company, raised more than $500,000 from investors, rented a huge factory, hired people, made tons of samples for reps, and never generated more than $200,000 a year in orders. Blodee discovered what other entrepreneurs found out— manufacturing is a tough business, the hardest to make go. And behind every successful manufacturing company must be a super sales force and a group of dedicated, professional representatives who can sell the product. Doing so takes salespeople, not just designers.

Although some of these failures can be blamed on a lack of capital, the root cause was management, not a shortage of funds. Lack of capital is often cited as an excuse for poor management, but in the end it is usually the people in a company that make the difference.

Examples of management failures usually can be found in enterprises that have grown rapidly. When inadequate management rears its head, the enterprise comes to a halt. These businesses not only stop growing, but they fail within a short period, too. Every rapidly growing business, regardless of whether it is service, retail, or manufacturing, can easily fall victim to this problem. All it takes is a founder/owner who cannot look at the company objectively.

The difficulties inherent in managing employees was one of the small business elements that Mike Goldberg weighed carefully before launching his enterprise. Employees meant that Mike would have to earn more, take on more clients, work more hours, and have more aggravation. He did not want that. Nor did he want the worries that came with a high overhead or cash-intensive enterprise. From the beginning, the young New York entrepreneur designed his business so it would be highly profitable, without employees, and with minimal risk and overhead.

His investment, just over $1,000, was a fraction of what Kirk and Helmers put into their restaurant and art supply store. Yet within a year Goldberg had made his investment back 100 times over as an advertising representative. (Advertising reps sell advertising space to clients in the publications they represent.)

The difference was that Goldberg selected a business that he knew something about. He knew he could run it with minimal overhead, without other employees, and it would carry an insignificant risk. For 15 years he had been

employed as an advertising representative for trade magazines, and he knew the business would work.

Dennis McCuistion, who started his own financial consulting firm with minimal expenditure, says the "successful
consultant has a choice. He can stay small or he can hire
and grow. You can make a good income either way, but the
choice is yours. You don't have to hire people."

Jerry Turner, who started a parking lot paving and striping business that will gross more than $2 million this year,
knew he could not avoid hiring employees.

> It's a pitfall, especially in a business like ours
> that is labor intensive. The one thing you have to do
> is watch them and make sure everyone knows what
> they are supposed to do, and there is a supervisor to
> make sure it is done. No employee is going to feel
> the same way you do about your business. As long as
> you remember that, you can avoid some of the pit-
> falls other owners have run into.

When Turner is out pursuing additional business and
his crew is working a job, his partner is there to ensure that
the work is done correctly, and vice versa. One of the
partners is always around checking up on things.

"Poor employees are only one of the pitfalls," says Turner.
"Undercapitalization can be a culprit, too." Running short
of capital is usually caused by a lack of knowledge. The less
you know, the more capital you require to run a company.
Experience equals capital. According to Turner:

> The more you have of one, the less you need of
> the other. "If you make a mistake in business, you
> can usually make up for it by spending capital. Ob-
> viously, the more experience you have, the less chance
> you have of making a mistake. Most failures happen
> because of a lack of experience. And that lack may

result in lost money, hiring the wrong person, or locating in the wrong area. You can't beat experience."

Poor Marketing Strategy

Odd as it may seem, some failures occur because the owner/creator neglects to find out if the business makes financial sense. Many people just plunge into an enterprise without researching it. A good example is the bright young West Coast entrepreneur who recently came up with a new innovative "bathtub" for cats. It held the animal painlessly in place, while the owner (or groomer) could bathe the cat.

It was an innovation that the industry sorely needed. Groomers, who make their living bathing animals, frequently have problems with cats. The new tub eliminates those difficulties, enabling groomers to be more productive—with less trauma to the animal. Another market would be the many veterinarians who have bathing facilities in their hospitals.

The tub's developer recognized these markets, but he wanted to sell to the public, because vets and groomers were a limited audience. When he started to market the tub to retail stores, however, he discovered it was priced too high. Vets or groomers—people who would use the tub professionally and could amortize its cost—were willing to pay $100 for a tub, but consumers were a different story.

He tried to lower the cost by designing new molds. Nothing worked, and he was not able to get the tub into a price category that would make it a mass-marketable item. Although it was an idea that filled a need, it did not make financial sense to the general public.

Finances are, of course, critical. Before launching a business, the owner should carefully ascertain sales, profits—and losses. Businesses differ radically in their financial requirements, and failure to recognize these differences has sunk more than one enterprise. The retailer is faced with overhead that consists of rent, merchandise (product), marketing, and employees. The manufacturer has product cost, packaging, shipping, marketing, co-op advertising, employees, and commissions. The service entrepreneur is most fortunate and usually faces only rent, telephone, fax, employees, and miscellaneous expenses.

Each of these businesses sells something different and requires different margins. Retailers usually double the cost of their goods to the end user. Manufacturers tack 50 percent (or more) onto the cost of their goods, and service providers have to carefully evaluate their time—

Type of Expense	Retailer	Manufacturer	Service
Produce Cost	X	X	
Packaging		X	
Shipping		X	
Co-op Advertising	X	X	
Commissions	X	X	X
Marketing	X	X	X
Employees	X	X	X
Distribution		X	
Miscellaneous Expense	X	X	X
Office Overhead	X	X	X
Fax	X	X	X
Telephone	X	X	X
Rent	X	X	X

This simple grid gives you a clue as to why service businesses are less likely to fail—they have fewer expenditures.

that's what they are selling. (In Chapter 6, pricing and billing techniques are covered in-depth.)

The inability of any of these businesspeople adequately to evaluate the cost of their goods and services can lead to financial disaster. And it frequently does. In their haste and enthusiasm for their enterprise, many businesspeople fail to price correctly. They forget an important part of the financial equation, and before they know it they are selling goods and services, but not making money.

Blind faith is another problem related to the pricing pitfall. Regardless of how much an entrepreneur loves a product and/or service, success is not a sure thing. For a business to take off, there has to be a need, marketing strategy, and, if the business is a product, distribution. Some of the best mousetraps ever designed never make it to the marketplace because they lack sales and distribution. Thousands of new products are launched every year, but only a small fraction make it.

THE PROBLEMS WITH HOT PRODUCTS

New companies with one product that suddenly becomes a success court disaster. For example, a few years ago a new record label released its first single. Within weeks the disc was getting airplay across the country and consumers began mobbing stores to get a copy.

From sales of just a few thousand a week, orders climbed to 10,000 to 15,000 a week. The head of the company was beside himself with joy as orders flooded in from every part of the country. As the company filled the orders and shipped, however, suppliers began to complain. They were not getting paid. The record pressing plant was owed several hundred thousand dollars, and the freight company that delivered the product to distributors was becoming anxious as well.

Records were selling, but no one was getting paid. Consumers were purchasing and paying for records, but the money never left the retailers' accounting rooms. In general, large retailers are slow to pay. In this case, the retailers know that if they are dealing with a major label—Capital, Columbia, RCA—they must pay promptly, or they will not receive additional product. But when they are purchasing product from a new label, a label with only one hit, there is no rush to pay unless the label suddenly comes up with another hit. This label did not. The pressing plant finally cut off credit, as did the trucking company. No one wanted to work with the record company.

Desperate, the company president turned to his distributors and pressed them for funds. Cash came in slowly. Distributors pay only when they are paid, and retailers were holding the funds or spending them with other record companies—companies with hot products that consumers were demanding.

Eventually the record company went bankrupt. It was sitting on a record that sold more than 5 million copies, but it could not pay its bills. The reality of retail had driven it to bankruptcy. By the time the large retailers paid what they owed, the label was out of business, and the creditors did the collecting.

Because of such scenarios, many new product developers want to distribute on their own. More than 20 years ago an aggressive young entrepreneur was traveling with his wife through San Francisco, when they saw a Volkswagen "bug" in the lane next to them. What amused both Don Kracke and his wife were the colorful flowers painted on both sides of the VW. They began to talk about the designs (all in the shape of flowers), and what a clever idea they were, and how popular flowers were in the Bay Area. That's when the idea hit them. Why not develop a product in the shape of a flower that could be affixed to a wall, car, garage, fence, or any structure? An attractive-looking flower . . . a flower they would call "Ricky-Ticky-Sticky."

Having an idea is one thing; bringing a product to market is entirely different. But the couple was determined. And they started the right way. First, they approached a manufacturer who agreed to make prototypes "on spec." If the product sold, they would give the manufacturing contract to him. Although speculative arrangements are still possible, the thin profit margin per product and enormous competition has diminished the number of manufacturers who want to take a chance on an untested product.

While the prototypes were being fabricated, the couple visited chains and retail outlets, searching for any similar competitive product. They also studied shelving, displays, and how similar products were merchandised in-store. Kracke knew the fastest way to failure would be to manufacture a product that needed a special display case or merchandiser. Stores will not invest in merchandisers, and if a manufacturer does not supply one, the product is not going to get displayed.

Kracke's idea was to use existing merchandisers to display his product. After visiting half a dozen outlets, it became apparent that the only place a Ricky-Ticky-Sticky could be merchandised and displayed was from a metal rack. The Sticky would be shrink-wrapped in plastic or cellophane, and a hole would be drilled at the top of the package so it could be slipped onto the arms of the rack.

Kracke's next step was to test-market price. He took several prototypes and started knocking on his neighbors' doors. He asked one question: "What would you be willing to pay for this package of Ricky-Ticky-Stickies?"

Market research does not require the skills of a brain surgeon. After an evening of questioning, Kracke and his wife came up with a feasible price. Now only one element remained in launching the product: distribution.

Kracke visited novelty distributors, who unanimously turned their backs on the new product. It did not have a track record, and they were unwilling to take on an item that had not proven itself. But how can a product prove itself if it has never been distributed? And how can a person get a distributor if distributors refuse to take on a line until it has been proven?

The couple encountered this obstacle 20 years ago, and today nothing has changed. Entrepreneurs with new products must prove their sales potential before a distributor will take them. For the most part, that means advertising, promotion, and creating demand—as Simple Green did.

The Krackes, however, did nothing of the sort. They came up with a scheme that worked then and can work today. They had a supply of Stickies made, researched a local department store, found it had racks in place, and made an appointment to see the purchasing agent. If they could sell the agent with their market studies and the apparent willingness of consumers to purchase the item, they believed he would agree to give it an in-store trial.

That's what happened. Kracke convinced the agent to give the product a chance. He put a dozen on one of the racks in-store. Slowly the item began to sell. Then it caught on. Within a week the agent was on the telephone, asking for a larger supply.

Within a few months other stores in the area had heard about the Stickies and they wanted them, too. Within a year the couple saw distribution of their product go from one West Coast city to thousands of retail outlets throughout the country.

For the next three years they sold Ricky-Ticky-Stickies as fast as they could make them. The item, which was a fad product, eventually died out, but not before Stickies accounted for more than $20 million in sales.

Happy ending? Not quite. The success of the Stickies is an example of why many manufactured products fail—even if they are successful. Kracke and his wife did not sell all $20 million worth of Stickies. In fact, they only sold $3 million. The other $17 million were "ripoffs," that is, virtual duplicates of the Stickies.

"Ripoffs," explains Kracke, who has marketed hundreds of products since then, "are commonplace. If you come up with a winner, you can expect knockoffs to emerge." Knockoffs are cheaper imitations of the real thing. IBM has its clones, and there is a big audience for them. The same was true for the Stickies. "Clones" emerged, and the Krackes' net for their three years of work was under $200,000.

SERVICE BUSINESSES: LESS DISASTER-PRONE?

While products have a high failure rate, service businesses have much less potential for disaster. Still, some service businesses have pitfalls. One is mail order. You might wonder: How can you miss? All you have to do is find the right product, send out sales letters, and sit back and wait for the dollars to roll in.

Nothing could be farther from the truth. Ask Chase Revel, *Entrepreneur* magazine's founder. He started the magazine with a $44 dollar mail order ad and built it into a multimillion-dollar publishing empire. Later he took another product, invested $700, and, once again, hit it big, this time with a business that grossed $6 million in just over a year.

Despite his success, Revel cautions there is more to mail order than picking a product. You have to be able to select and test lists, and write convincing copy. Remember, you must persuade people to trust you. They have to put their hard-earned dollars in an envelope and send it through the mail to a stranger. That is not an easy thing to get people to do.

Copywriting and picking a winning product are only

part of the mail order mix. Knowledge of the industry is another, equally as important, part of the business. For instance, even if the product developed has appeal, mail order entrepreneurs frequently make a mistake in picking lists that they are going to rent. They may, for example, have a product that they know physicians would buy. They may contact a list broker, who tells them he has a list with 100,000 doctors' names on it. They buy the list, mail it, and nothing happens.

What happened? Why did the mailing fail? It could be a combination of factors—wrong letter, wrong product, or, wrong list. Just because people are on a list does not mean they are mail order responsive.

Revel estimates that as many as 400,000 people a year enter the mail order fray. When he ran *Entrepreneur*, the magazine's biggest selling business start-up manual was "mail order." The failure rate is anyone's guess, but the former publisher says he would not be surprised if "more than 95 percent of those who enter fail. Most people view it as a simple business, one where they do not have to go to the office or know anything about the customer. All they need is a product. As you can see, nothing could be farther from the truth."

The cost of launching a product or mail order business is another reason for the high failure rate. If a product retails for $24, you can bet the manufacturer has an investment of approximately $4. The cat "bather," which retailed for $100, cost the manufacturer about $20. The manufacturer's cost represents the dollars needed to fabricate the product—not market it. In mail order, marketing costs are extremely high, and in order to make a profit a mail order entrepreneur has to price their product about five times the cost, because of the high marketing expenditure.

For example, aside from the actual product, the mail order entrepreneur has a budget for a variety of items ranging from copywriting, brochure production, advertising, fulfillment (mailing), customer service and clerical help, and cost of returned and/or damaged goods.

The least costly mail order product is paper. A "how to" book or brochure. Paper does not spoil, nor is it particularly costly to mail. And, the entrepreneur can limit his investment by not producing thousands of products until he is sure (via advertisements and response) that the public wants to buy it. A mail order book that costs $1 a copy to print, can cost tens of thousands of dollars in marketing.

Now let's examine a typical service business. A distribution representative can be launched for less than $1,000; a maid service, for less than $2,000; a janitorial service, for less than $3,000; advertising rep for the same; parking lot striper for under $10,000.

The capital required for these enterprises is less, and so is the risk. Those offering products and mail order items are trying to sell something new and unproven. Human nature does not look kindly upon the new or unusual. But service businesses offer the familiar: cleaning, consulting, representation, and the like. And astute providers of services always market something they know about. That's one of the keys to the success of fail-safe businesses.

HOW TO SELECT A BUSINESS

Revel's success with *Entrepreneur* is illustrative of the need to select a business you know about. Before he started the magazine, Revel had been involved in 18 different small businesses, all but one of which was successful. He knew about small business and in the magazine could offer valuable advice.

To avoid business failure if you are considering entering the service field, you should have experience in the industry, just as Revel had. Do not try to make the enterprise new and original—remember, consumers/buyers dislike the new and revolutionary. Add a new twist, but make it evolutionary. Revolutions fail.

Revel used that approach when he founded *Entrepreneur*. To differentiate the magazine from the dozens of other business opportunity publications in the field, each issue featured a complete, how-to, practical guide on how to duplicate an existing, successful small business. He told readers everything from site location to marketing. None of the other publications gave in-depth information. It was an evolutionary difference—that worked.

Revel's venture into the business opportunity expo field is another example of an evolutionary business. Dozens of promoters were putting on successful business opportunity and franchise shows, but Revel designed one with a new twist—seminars.

The seminars became one of the most popular aspects of the *Entrepreneur* expositions. For more than four years the publication ran one show a month in a different city. Each expo was loaded with seminars. The shows helped the publication build circulation, mail order base, and cash flow. Revel took a proven concept (the shows), added to it (heavy advertising and promotion), differentiated his product slightly (the seminars), and came up with a winning formula that helped increase his sales to more than $15 million.

The franchise system does the same thing. It takes a proven concept (one store or unit) and duplicates the concept across the country. That's how good franchisors operate. They test and prove the concept on a small scale and then expand it. They do not make units different; the strength of a franchise is in keeping every outlet and its operation procedures identical. They emulate the success of the first units, and if something is added, it is an evolutionary product/item, not revolutionary. No one addition changes the concept of the enterprise. That's exactly what Revel did with the business expos. He took a proven winner (his business expos) and duplicated it across the country, much as franchisor would do.

Moving slowly and giving customers what they are familiar with is the way "failure-proof" businesses operate. Businesses that defy this rule and offer revolutionary new concepts are prone to failure because people are not open to change. That's one of the reasons most political incumbents are returned to office. People like the status quo. There are, in fact, numerous cases where incumbents actually violated their oaths and duties and were still returned to office. And, believe it or not, voters have even returned dead politicians to office.

Certainly there are occasions when a new, revolutionary product or service will break through. Look at Kracke's Ricky-Ticky-Stickies or the Pet Rock. Notice, however, these are items that did not last. They were fads.

As a prospective businessperson, you will do better if you examine what products and services are out there now. Ask yourself: Which do I know about? Can I make a slight change, or put my own twist to it, so it will be a successful new business? If you can, you may be creating a "failure-proof" enterprise.

In the mid-1980s Van Pler & Tissany showed just how profitable the evolutionary approach could be. For years ambitious, creative mail order entrepreneurs had been trying to sell the public on buying synthetic diamonds. For the most part, they were unsuccessful. Consumers did not buy.

Van Pler studied the approach that previous mail order marketers had taken. Each had constructed quality, effective mail order ads—that failed to return a profit. The firms had placed full-page ads in publications such as the *National Enquirer*, *Star*, and other mass-marketed tabloids. Nothing worked. Why? To Van Pler the answer was relatively simple, and the company proved it with its first ad.

The mail order entrepreneurs had concentrated on trying to market the synthetics to people who could not afford the real thing. It made sense—or did it? Would, for instance, the wife of a laborer making just a few dollars an hour over minimum wage be interested in wearing a three-carat CZ diamond? Certainly she would love to have the real thing, but there is practicality and reality. How many of her friends would believe the stone was real? They know her husband works for relatively low wages, so how could he possibly afford a real three-carat gem? He could not. The stone must be a phony.

Husbands and wives of lower-income workers understood that better than those marketing the CZs. They read the tabloids but shied away from the offers. Van Pler theorized that the stones would never sell in great quantities to the mass market. Instead, the company took a slightly different tack. Ads were structured and placed in the *Wall Street Journal*, *Forbes*, and *Fortune*. These were publications with upscale readers—doctors, lawyers, CPAs, professionals. These were the people, theorized Van Pler, who would not hesitate buying a CZ because no one would question the gem's authenticity. Everyone knew they could afford the real thing.

The professionals had a secondary motive. Besides being able to give gifts that looked valuable, they did not have to worry about theft. There was no insurance problem.

Van Pler launched its campaign, one that went on to gross millions of dollars despite the firm's internal problems, and one that illustrates how a small but significant change can make a major difference in a small business venture.

SMALL CHANGES ARE EASIER TO SELL

Small changes impact the business enterprise of consultants, too. The consultant who examines a client company and proceeds to recommend revolutionary changes will not have that company long as a client. If there is too much to be fixed, as illustrated by the number of revolutionary changes proposed, the consultant is really saying that the senior/top managers are in the wrong.

When this happens, senior managers begin looking at each other and realize the consultant is blaming them. That brings on an immediate defensive response and a demand for a new consultant.

Successful consultants do not attempt to change everything, even if it does need changing. They work on small bits and pieces. They nibble at the larger problem and eventually get to it by building up a series of small changes.

One case that illustrates the importance of bringing people along slowly with evolutionary changes is the "brick oven."

A young West Coast entrepreneur created a product that improved the efficiency of an oven by 20 percent and made the food taste better. The product was an ordinary clay brick. The brick was preheated in an oven, and absorbed the heat before the item to be cooked was placed on it.

Once the food was set on the brick, several things happened. The brick cooked the food faster and more evenly. It helped retain the flavorful juices, because the food cooked rapidly. The inventor thought he had a winner and was about to put together a half-hour informercial, but he wanted to test it first.

He had samples manufactured and supplied them to housewives, chefs, and other consumers. After they used it, the inventor asked one question: Would you buy it? Overwhelmingly, everyone answered yes.

The inventor wanted to test the product once more. He put together a direct mail piece that would go to people who had previously bought culinary items through the mail. He believed the match would be perfect. What better crowd to test the viability of the item?

Despite the polished, professional-quality mailing piece, his response was poor. In evaluating the product and mailing afterward, the answer suddenly hit him. Everyone who tried the clay brick loved it, but in real life you cannot let people try your product before you sell it to them. It's impossible.

Without trying the brick for themselves, consumers did not believe it would work. Although the inventor had a better mousetrap, he discovered that people did not beat a path to his door.

Despite horror stories of products and services that have not made it, failure is not an integral part of small business. For a long time, the view has been that four out of five new U.S. businesses fail within five years. That's a dismal statistic and reason for anyone to think twice before starting his or her enterprise.

However, entrepreneurs take heart. Those numbers are not accurate. The failure rate for small business is far less than one might imagine. Recently economist Bruce Kirchoff of the New Jersey Institute of Technology produced a study in which he traced the success/failure of more than 800,000 businesses that were started in 1977–78. He tracked them for more than eight years, and found that more than half continued to thrive long after the five-year mark. And, according to the study, only 18 percent of those 800,000 plus actually failed.

Why the discrepancy between Kirchoff and government studies? Revel explains:

> It's simple. When an entrepreneur closes a business, it is not always because he is failing. He may be bored or tired, or he may sell it, or switch to another industry. Simply putting a padlock on the door does not mean failure.
>
> More important are the statistics. If four out of five small businesses failed within the first five years,

in order to have the number of successful businesses we have today, everyone in this country would have had to start one. And that includes children under the age of five! The statistics do not add up.

What is clear, however, is that small businesses can fail, especially if they violate or ignore the key elements required to make a business a success. But owning your own small business can be rewarding. If you select the correct enterprise and put in place the right operating procedures, the business also can be "failure-proof." In the next chapter we examine some of the many businesses that have, indeed, proven to be "failure-proof" and what characteristics they have in common.

2

Characteristics of "Failure-Proof" Businesses

What makes a small business "failure-proof"? Obviously, the entrepreneurial characteristics of the owners count, but these are not the only elements that determine why some businesses seem to hit gold almost from the day they are created.

Consider the following businesses. They are in industries ranging from consulting to grooming, yet they all have several common characteristics. And each has become a "failure-proof" enterprise.

Tony Walton—Computer Consultant

After three years with a Fortune 500 computer manufacturer, Tony Walton was somewhat surprised when his supervisor sat down and told him he was being laid off. Walton had seen it happen to others, but he never imagined he would be one of the victims. He had put in countless overtime, had been given a bonus for a suggestion he had made that saved the company thousands of dollars, and had been told more than once that he was unquestionably one of the top computer repair specialists in the firm.

Walton was only one of many to be let go. First he thought he would try to find another job before his severance and unemployment ran out. He had heard too many horror stories about managers who waited too long and, before they knew what happened, had exhausted their benefits and still were without a job.

Within hours after he was given his final paycheck at the traditional exit interview, Walton began to plan. Questions gnawed at him. Would he wind up with another company, do the same superior job, and end up being laid off? He was not ready for another devastating experience. Like his coworkers, Walton had plans to send his resume and hit as many prospective employers as possible. In the back of his mind, however, there was the thought that regardless of whom he worked for, the cycle would be repeated.

Then fate took a hand. Prior to being laid off, Walton had been helping a former classmate who had opened a small business. The man needed a computerized accounting and sales system, in addition to word processing capability, but knew little about computers or software.

Walton had spent countless hours talking to his classmate about current and future computer needs. Based on their conversations, he designed the system, priced it, explained it, and trained his friend's personnel on how to use it.

The evening of his layoff, Walton sat across the table from his wife, discussing his options and their future. A call from his classmate interrupted the conversation, but it also opened up an entirely new career for Walton, a career he had not even thought about—his own business.

During the next month, while he continued searching for a new position, Walton worked for his friend on a part-time consulting basis. Through the man's recommendations, Walton soon found himself with three additional small business clients. By the end of the second month, Walton had a half-dozen clients who regularly called on him for repair and design assistance. Suddenly it occurred to him: Why work for someone else? He had already laid the groundwork for his own profitable business.

Lana McKendry—Manufacturer's Representative

Lana McKendry had a similar experience. She was a waitress in San Diego, and one day she sat down and began scolding herself. "I just had to get something going," she recalls, "and being a waitress was going nowhere."

McKendry started looking. She landed a job at a large lumber company and was soon hired away by one of the giant new home service centers that were popping up across the country. This particular chain specialized in homebuilding materials.

"I didn't know anything about the business, and I was earning less money than when I was a waitress, but I knew there was a future," McKendry says.

The future became reality when McKendry became fascinated by the process by which manufacturers got their wares into the giant home centers. They had a tough sell, and only a few manufacturers had a local representative to handle their lines and sell the centers on stocking their goods.

Eventually McKendry decided she could act as that representative, or rep. She could work for the manufacturers, sell centers on carrying their lines, and take care of the in-store displays as well. She left the center and opened her own business. That was seven years ago.

Mike Goldberg—Independent Advertising Representative

Mike Goldberg became a rep as well. Instead of handling goods, he entered the advertising field, where he sold his services as a space salesman for magazines. Here's what Goldberg has to say.

I had been an advertising rep for years and was employed by a variety of publications, but in the back of my mind, I always wanted to do my own thing.

One day I decided to try it—by taking one step at a time. I sent letters to several smaller publications that I knew did not employ in-house representatives; they were too small.

I found numerous books within the same industry that were noncompeting. Some were quite large. For instance, in the pet industry if I represented a bird publication, I would not take on a competing one. I could, however, represent a dog and cat magazine, or a grooming publication. None was competing, yet I could concentrate on the same industry and sell for a variety of books.

I picked the [pet] industry because I knew it, and I believe the same thing could be done in any other field with any group of magazines. It works, publishers need help. Especially those with smaller, niche magazines that cannot afford to hire in-house advertising sales help. From my standpoint there were definite benefits. I could represent an entire line in one industry.

Most pet industry publications were national, and they were all interested in having someone who would work on commission—no in-house health or benefit costs or salary was involved. It worked for Goldberg and the magazines.

Kendall Shurcut—Grooming Salon Owner

Kendall Shurcut found something that worked in the pet industry, too. After graduating high school, Shurcut began to examine his options. For months he was unable to focus on any specific opportunity, until he went to work as a clerk in a pet store. Shurcut enjoyed working with animals, and he found a natural rapport with pet owners. They both cared about animals.

While at the pet store, he began to notice several things about the animal owners he met. All were willing to spend more money on their animal than they would on themselves. But, despite their willingness to spend, when it came to pet supplies they had limited knowledge, and they relied heavily on the clerks to guide their choices.

Inside the store was a grooming salon, and the three groomers who worked six days a week rarely had a break between the dogs and cats they were bathing. Shurcut knew the fees and how much the salon charged for each bath and its actual labor and material costs. Grooming had an incredible potential, especially if groomers priced their services correctly, targeted the right audience, and located in a convenient center. Shurcut eventually did with his own salon.

Ginny Anderson—Mobile Groomer

Ginny Anderson worked in a grooming salon, too, and saw the same needs that Shurcut had discovered. Anderson, however, decided to take grooming one step farther. Instead of opening a storefront, she found a way to avoid rent. She took a used van, equipped it with bathing and grooming supplies along with two small tubs, and became a mobile groomer. The mobile groomer comes to the home, plugs electrical appliances into the consumer's outlets, and bathes the animal in a van that is parked in the consumer's driveway.

Dennis McCuistion—Banking Industry Consultant

Dennis McCuistion, a longtime banking industry employee, saw the industry going through dramatic changes in the 1980s.

"Few industries downsized as severely as banking. Closed branches were everywhere, but despite the contraction, there was opportunity," he recalls.

Almost from the day he left his employer, McCuistion began to receive calls from former banking associates. McCuistion is a troubleshooter—a banking and financial specialist who could come into an enterprise, spot the problem, and recommend the solution.

McCuistion discovered that because so many banks had downsized and cut employees, many who were employed were not as qualified as he was. Some could not even read financial statements. They needed help, and his telephone began to ring. Those initial calls were enough to convince him that his consulting practice could not miss. It was virtually "failure-proof."

Delia Ornaz—Cleaning Service Owner

Delia Ornaz came to the United States five years ago and found it difficult to get any work other than odd jobs paying minimum wages. She talked to her friends, and they were in the same position. It was difficult to make a living.

One Saturday morning she was opening her mail when she saw the Val Pak direct mail insert. It was from a maid service, and it offered a 10 percent discount for anyone who called the following week to have her house cleaned.

Ornaz studied the rates. Even with the discount, the fee was $45 for a four-hour shift, more than double what she was making. Ornaz called the maid service and applied for work.

For the next six months, she worked as a housecleaner and saw the opportunity. Most maids went into a home, went about their business, and left without saying much to the customers. Some cleaning services even requested that the customers leave while the maid cleaned. Ornaz could see the fallacy in the approach. The maid never had a chance to built rapport with the person whose home she was cleaning.

Ornaz recognized that because of this lack of rapport, people switched maids and maid services frequently. She also saw that many of the maids were unsupervised and did much as they pleased. Many watched soap operas when the customers left, and the cleaning jobs were always half-hearted.

Ornaz's approach was different. As long as she was in a home, she cleaned, and cleaned thoroughly. While many of her fellow maids were switched almost weekly to different houses, she began to build a solid clientele. Because of Ornaz's thoroughness, customers refused to accept a different maid. Before long, Ornaz had a solid, steady stream of customers who kept her busy five days a week.

In Ornaz's opinion, the business was easy. Once you had customers, you could keep them forever, if you treated them right and cleaned the property thoroughly. Ornaz did, and less than a year after she began working for the maid service she had opened her own cleaning service.

Jay Horoki—Janitorial Service Owner

Jay Horoki saw the same opportunity in janitorial work. There was little communication between the janitorial company and the client. Once the contract had been obtained, the owner of the building or the tenant seldom saw the janitorial people again.

Many jobs were done is a slipshod manner, too. Janitorial helpers worked graveyard (midnight to 8 A.M.) or a late-evening shift, and most were transients. They were paid poorly and were never around long. Horoki envisioned starting a company and building a stable group of workers who were well paid and could see the benefits from being loyal to it. He also saw the importance of communicating with clients, not only to see if the job was being done to the customers' satisfaction but in order to get to know the tenants (and landlord) and hope for referrals.

Jerry Turner—Parking Lot Striping and Paving

Jerry Turner spent several years working for an entrepreneur in the southwest United States, who specialized in striping and paving parking lots. Jerry discovered, however, that his boss seldom generated repeat business. In order to survive, the company's owner was constantly pursuing prospective new clients.

The reason his boss failed in attracting repeat customers (and referrals) was obvious to Jerry—shoddy workmanship and poor quality materials. Within a few months after they would pave or strip a lot, the ground would begin to crack and the lines wear off. His boss "guaranteed" the work, but the guarantees always expired just before the jobs fell apart.

Turner often wondered what would happen if his boss turned to quality instead of the shoddy workmanship and materials. Several years later he found out first-hand when he started his own company; a company built on a foundation of quality.

Today, the majority of Turner's $2 million in striping and paving business comes from one source—referral.

EIGHT CHARACTERISTICS OF "FAILURE-PROOF" BUSINESSES

Although these entrepreneurs entered diverse industries, their businesses all shared several characteristics, characteristics that are typical of "failure-proof" enterprises.

1. Industry experience. Every one of the owners worked in the industry before they started their own business. They knew the field, and they knew the pitfalls.

2. Service businesses. These entrepreneurs stayed away from retail and manufacturing enterprises, which are traditionally capital intensive and loaded with pitfalls.

3. Low start-up. Each of these businesses required little capital. Virtually every "failure-proof" enterprise in this book requires relatively little capital. The most capital intensive was Jerry Turner's striping business, which ran just over $10,000. Putting a great deal of capital into an enterprise does not guarantee success.

4. Low overhead. After starting, none of the entrepreneurs saw the need for fancy, expensive offices. They all kept their office space and overhead reasonable. Their object was to be profitable, not project an expensive image.

5. Definite need. This is a key requirement for every business: People must *need* the product or service. If they do not, regardless of the marketing effort, it will not work. Each of these entrepreneurs determined that there was a need before they opened their doors.

6. Niche enterprise. These entrepreneurs did not try to be all things to all people; rather they concentrated on a specific segment of an industry. Specialized businesses do much better than those that try to appeal to everyone.

7. Steady growth. Every one of these businesses has an upward growth pattern. They are services that are in demand today and in the foreseeable future.

8. Economic stimulus. While the economy may impact a number of enterprises negatively, with most of these businesses, economic downturns can have positive effects. Notice many of them solve time and convenience problems. Others assist companies that have had to downsize and outsource.

The entrepreneurs who founded these businesses took certain initial steps, too. In other words, they answered market research questions *before* they invested, not after. They went by facts, not gut instinct. Each determined if the business was "right." In other words, they asked: Is there a place for it? Is there a demand for the service or product? Tony Walton saw the need that small business people had for a computer repair specialist; Lana McKendry and Mike Goldberg understood the problems that manufacturers and publishers had in generating business despite having excellent products; Kendall Shurcut could see the time and convenience needs of people with animals; Delia Ornaz recognized the demands put on people who no longer had time to clean because they were breadwinners; Jay Horoki saw that tenants and landlords were getting shoddy service; and Dennis McCuistion recognized the huge need that downsizing had created in the banking industry.

The research was not sophisticated, but it gave each businessperson insight into the demands there would be for his or her services. Walton's research came in the form of calls from prospective clients. By their inquiries, he could see that there was a niche he could fill. While thousands of computer repair specialists and programmers were unemployed and trying to start their own businesses, in their panic to find employment most ignored the small business owner. They were after large companies that could afford to pay hefty monthly retainers. Or they wanted to work for a major corporation in order to collect health and pension benefits.

Walton cared about benefits but they were not his prime motivation. What he saw was *opportunity*. Small business owners did not have access to competent computer expertise. If they needed a program or repair assistance, they would call the equipment manufacturer or the service company. Once their warranties ran out, they faced horrendous costs.

Walton offered an option. He did not ask for a retainer, which most small businesses would have trouble coming up with. Small businesses do not usually have excess capital. To Walton, the business opportunities were worth far more than retainers.

Retainers have advantages and disadvantages. The advantage is, of course, up-front money. The disadvantage is that once clients pay, they expect something. They have to see the consultant. If the consultant does not show up, clients begin to wonder if he or she is earning the retainer. It doesn't take long before clients begin to wonder if the consultant is even worth the retainer.

Because he did not demand money up-front, Walton did not face any of these suspicions. Few of his competitors operated in a similar manner, despite the obvious fact that most small business owners could not afford retainers.

Walton's success was spurred on by another factor. He is in an industry where technology is constantly changing. Today's computer is obsolete tomorrow. Parts are hard to get, and technicians who understand those changes and when a business should consider replacing hardware (and software) are hard to find. Technology paved the way for Walton's business, as it has done so many times before. New and improved products created opportunity for him.

Technology does the same thing in most industries. It makes some equipment obsolete (along with some workers), but improvements always offer new opportunities. Entrepreneurs looking for opportunity keep their eyes on industries that are undergoing rapid technological change.

In McKendry's case, the opportunity was obvious, too, although the business opportunities were being created not by technology but by distribution changes. The huge home centers were squeezing out smaller retailers, and manufacturers could see their outlets shrinking. In many cases, the home centers bought directly from manufacturers at distributor cost. That meant manufacturers had to deal directly with the centers. If they refused, their lines never made it into the stores. Manufacturers were caught in a bind. They needed to reach the home centers, but their distributors could not help.

McKendry saw the need for a service business to solve manufacturers' problems. Although McKendry deals with manufacturers who produce products for home building centers, there are hundreds of manufacturers in other industries who need distribution and sales help as well. Almost every industry is going through a distribution change. Some of the change is due to the creation of so-called superstores, huge stores that dwarf traditional retail outlets with the amount of goods carried, while other change is simply a reflection of downsizing and cost-cutting measures. Retailers everywhere are trying to improve profit margins. That means buying for less—buying for distributor price.

Some industries are in a state of flux, while others are chaotic. Both cases offer opportunity for the astute entrepreneur. Why? Change breeds opportunity.

Mike Goldberg's decision to become a rep for publications within the same industry was dictated by market changes, too. He could see the shrinking profit margins of most publications. Some of the loss came because industries were not advertising as much; in some cases the loss was caused by advertisers putting their money into in-store displays, promotional incentives, or other media rather than print ads.

Either way, the magazines had to cut back, and that meant fewer advertising sales personnel at a time when more were needed in order to drum up more business. Goldberg solved the problem by offering publishers a viable option: generating more advertisements with less overhead. What more could they ask? The same is true of other industries that have been forced to cut back. Layoffs and hard times represent opportunities for entrepreneurs.

The success of Dennis McCuistion's consulting venture was virtually assured by the massive restructuring of the banking industry. Those with McCuistion's skills were laid off because they were usually higher-priced employees. The people who were left could not handle the complex financial requirements—which left a huge gap for people like McCuistion to fill.

In all four enterprises—computer service, manufacturer's rep, advertising rep, and financial consulting—opportunities were created because of changes in technology and the way people do business. Change typically opens the door to new opportunities. Even in Kendall Shurcut's case, change had an impact.

Shurcut's services were in demand because of the changes in the working family. Instead of one breadwinner, almost every family has two. People have less leisure time, and even less time for bathing a pet. Consumers want convenience, and Shurcut's enterprise offered that in the service it offered and the convenient location. Consumers could drop off their animals in the morning; Shurcut would bathe and groom them and hold them until the owners picked up the pets after work.

Tony Walton's opportunity came through change, too. Companies had downsized, and smaller enterprises could not afford full-time computer help; nor could they even pay retainers. The profit squeeze has been on in all fields for several years and will continue well into the 1990s.

COMPETITION—HOW BIG A FACTOR?

Jay Horoki carved a niche in a traditional industry, one with an abundance of competition. But he—and Delia Ornaz—proved that competition has little to do with whether a business is profitable or not. It is the people who run it and the service that is given.

Americans will go out of their way to hire a company or individual who offers superior service. Few companies do. Most entrepreneurs are in and out—they get the job done and run. Horoki and Ornaz both recognized the need for someone to come in and do a thorough job and provide the ultimate in service. Consumers are willing to pay a premium for such service. And customers will switch from companies that do a poorer job without a second thought. The service ethic is one of the most critical characteristics of "failure-proof" businesses. It distinguishes every one of these enterprises from the competition.

Nordstrom's has built an enormously successful chain of department stores through its emphasis on service. In most cases, goods are more expensive at Nordstrom's, but consumers accept the higher price in exchange for the superb service.

Every prospective service entrepreneur should take a tip from Nordstrom's. You can charge more—if your service is the best. A customer's worst nightmare is having to return merchandise or being dissatisfied with a job. Alleviate those concerns, and you have the foundation for a failure-proof enterprise.

Quality work produces more than a steady income—it leads to an endless stream of referrals, more business and higher profits.

Opportunities abound in every industry. Several of the businesses discussed in this book are in the pet industry, and for good reason. Over the past 10 to 15 years and the ups and downs of recessions, the pet industry has not only survived but continued to grow and prosper. People love their pets and in many cases are more willing to spend on the pets than on themselves.

Thanks to downsizing, outsourcing has emerged and changed the face of American business. Outsourcing—subcontracting work to others—is not a new concept, especially in the manufacturing field. H. Ross Perot, however, applied the concept of outsourcing to a new and rapidly changing field.

When Perot left IBM to form Electronic Data Systems (EDS) more than 30 years ago, computer technology was racing ahead, much as it is today. Users of data processing systems could not keep up with the rapid change. Perot saw an opportunity to provide trained data processing technicians and programmers to develop and operate customized systems for certain business users. He developed the expertise and sold it to businesses and organizations that lacked the internal resources to develop it. It was outsourcing, and the beginning of a new era in the computer industry—an era that since has spread to every industry in the United States.

Among the more common outsourced functions (and opportunities):

- Automation systems
- Computer network maintenance
- Communication networks
- High-priced, skilled executives
- Food services
- Legal services
- Mailroom automation and services
- Office maintenance and cleaning
- Payroll processing
- Relocation services
- Security
- Temporary help
- Travel services

SEARCH FOR "CORE BUSINESS"

As a rule, most business today is trying to get back to its "core business." A furniture retailer's core business is, for example, selling furniture. A department store's core business is selling whatever goods are within the store. A bank's core business is lending money. But in the rapid expansion of the 1970s and 1980s, many enterprises added lines. Some furniture retailers spent huge amounts of capital investing in data processing departments, while some department stores did the same. Banks got into real estate and other types of investments. These enterprises moved away from their area of expertise in hopes of increasing sales and profits.

Yet in the 1990s, the movement is back to the core. Insurance companies are concentrating on doing one thing— selling insurance. Real estate firms sell real estate. Foodmakers are into food. Most enterprises have divested themselves of departments or divisions that go beyond the core and now are buying those services from outsiders— those who provide outsourcing services. The "get back to the core" trend will probably stay with us throughout the 1990s.

Downsizing and the return to core businesses have created tremendous opportunities. Companies and organizations have fewer personnel to handle jobs other than what the firm's main business is. In the case of large home centers, for example, the emphasis is on selling. These centers do not have the time or bodies to place, stack, and display goods. They want help, yet they do not want representatives only to come through, place their merchandise, display it, and leave. Companies want suppliers—manufacturers and others—to help manage in-store products and displays.

A recent cover story in *Inc.* magazine detailed this phenomena. The article pointed out that many manufacturers are focusing on current clients and providing them with more services, instead of simply trying to generate new customers. They are closely examining the needs of these clients and using many of their own (the manufacturer's) sales personnel to answer those needs.

Business Interiors, an office furniture manufacturer that provides upscale office furniture to large home centers, realized that expensive furniture would not be suitable for many of its customers. For example, at the time Texas was going through a downturn in business and expensive furnishings were not in demand. Therefore, Business Interiors began to expand into other areas, areas from which its customers (the retail centers that sold to offices) could generate revenue.

The company added renting, refurbishing, and repairing furniture for its Texas clients. The strategy has paid off. Business Interiors president John Sample explains: "Forget what we sell. Let's ask customers what they want and organize ourselves around that."

Heresy—that's how this approach would have been viewed a few years back. Today, however, the numbers of sales outlets are shrinking, and those that remain are growing immensely. Wise manufacturers understand the need to get more involved with retailers. The closer the involvement, the greater dependence the seller will have on the manufacturer and the higher the assurance of reorders. What the mail order marketers knew years ago—that you can generate 50 percent or more in repeat sales from existing customers—is beginning to hit home in other industries.

The G&F/Bose arrangement well illustrates growing dependence on outside suppliers. G&F is a small manufacturer of molded plastic products, and Bose is an acoustic speaker maker that utilizes G&F products in its line. Bose asked if G&F would assign a full-time employee to work at its plant; this would eliminate the need for a G&F salesperson to call on Bose. By working with the full-timer devoted to its account only, Bose would save significant monies because it would not have to utilize a purchasing agent's time to price and order goods. G&F would benefit by having someone on-site who could order goods immediately (when needed) and it did not have to assign a salesperson to the account. Both parties benefitted. G&F's business increased, and Bose's costs dropped.

Lana McKendry recognized these trends, and although her rep business was nowhere near the size of that of Bose or G&F, the same principles apply. Retailers are looking for help. They want a relationship. McKendry built one and in doing so she has established a "failure-proof" business.

McKendry not only obtains the order from the home center, but her company deals with any defective or returned merchandise, handles the inventory, and makes sure the products are properly displayed. No home center personnel are involved, and someone from McKendry's firm is usually in every store every week.

This procedure saves the center money and enables McKendry's company to build and retain a close relationship with each of its clients.

Mike Goldberg's advertising rep business is in demand, too. "But you have to know the industry. I went into the pet field because of my experience. Someone who is in the automotive, food, or other industry could do the same."

In selecting an industry, Goldberg looked at one other thing. "Is the industry recession-proof? Or, at the very least, will it be one of the last industries impacted in the event of a downturn?"

The pet industry, for instance, continues to grow despite the economy. Grooming is related to the pet field. Expenditures continue to rise as households spend more each year on getting their pet bathed and groomed, because most households have two breadwinners. As the economy gets tighter, the marketplace will consist of more working families, and the demands for grooming services will grow. Kendall Shurcut recognized this need and is benefiting from it.

Ginny Anderson is benefitting from the lack of time consumers have and their search for more convenient services. By driving to the home, her mobile grooming service is one of the most convenient. And it is an enormous time-saver, too.

Anderson launched her mobile shop about five years ago, and today will service as many as eight clients a day, with an average grooming price of close to $40. (Mobile groomers command a higher fee because of the convenience of the service.)

Being mobile has tremendous advantages for owners. Although there is an initial outlay for an appropriately equipped van, there is no rent for a storefront and the electric bill is drastically reduced because the equipment is plugged into the consumer's outlets. Rent and electricity are usually a groomer's two greatest expenses, and mobile enterprises have them well under control.

The mobile groomer has the advantage of operating without hiring assistants, too. Because the van can visit and bathe only one animal at a time, there is no need for an assistant, unless a specialist, who only does grooming (but no bathing) is hired. In that case, the specialist gets a percentage (around 60 percent) of the grooming fee and works as an outside service, which saves the owner of the grooming service employment taxes.

Location is critical for retailers but far less important for service business owners. Retail, of course, must have a good location with constant traffic. In the consulting field, location is seldom important, because clients do not select consultants because they "drove by" and saw them. Usually, consultants get in the door or are hired because of reputation and reference. Clients don't visit consultants. Consultants do the calling.

Tony Walton, the computer consultant, operates out of his garage. He has remodeled it, put in computer banks, and set up a desk and telephone. Dennis McCuistion, the financial consultant, works from his home, too. Lana McKendry, the manufacturer's rep, has an office that has never been visited by a client. She travels throughout 11 states, and the clients expect to see her at their place of business. Mike operates out of his apartment; Jay has an office in a small commercial development; Delia operates with an answering service and so does Ginny.

Location is important for Kendall Shurcut's dog grooming business. He needed to be near an affluent area with a storefront that offered easy access. He located in a strip center, just a few minutes from where most of his clients lived.

Each of these people maintains a relatively low overhead. Years ago it was fashionable to have an expensive, fancy office where present and prospective customers could drop in anytime. Things have changed now. Clients don't have the luxury of extra time for socializing. Downsizing has taken care of that. Few even have time for a casual lunch, thus there is no need for an exclusive office or storefront.

Overhead is tightly controlled in these "failure-proof" ventures, mainly because of the lack of client expectations. Entrepreneurs who rent exclusive, expensive suites of offices are wasting their capital—unless they are trying to sell financial products or something similar.

Most "failure-proof" businesses studied have another common characteristic: They prefer to keep employees to a minimum. Some would rather avoid hiring than grow the business. The reasons are obvious: worker's compensation, taxes, and the growing number of lawsuits between employees and employer. Entrepreneurs have enough to worry about without frivolous lawsuits. Whenever possible, they limit employment. This policy does not severely curtail their income, either. Walton can make a six-figure income without assistance. The same is true of McKendry (she has a partner), and Goldberg. McCuistion has a small staff (three), while Shurcut hires two to three groomers to assist in the shop.

Walton could expand, hire additional computer consultants, and generate more business. But in consulting, problems develop when the founder/owner is no longer doing the work. Aside from personnel difficulties, clients expect the person who sells them to do the job. They do not want an assistant, regardless of that person's competence, to be their prime contact.

The consultant who sells the client is going to be the individual with the customer rapport. Bill Johnson, who started a "failure-proof" accounting firm (more than 80 percent of his services is in consulting, not in tax returns or financial statements), limited his firm to 26 employees. Johnson's profits have soared, despite the fact he turns down business. "With 26 of us, everyone knows everyone else. It's more of a family than a company. I like it that way. I could probably make much more money if we expanded, but I prefer a manageable enterprise where you are not a slave to overhead."

CONTROL OF EXPENSES

Walton explains: That's one of the advantages I saw in the way I structured my business. Large companies are constantly watching expenses and overhead. With your own business, you can control things. The profits are greater, too. I don't want to worry about employees. If I did expand, chances are I would not be making much more, because of the additional insurance and worker's compensation costs.

McCuistion shares those thoughts. He has had the opportunity to expand and bring other consultants into his business, but he has declined.

It is much easier to manage. If you are in a business that requires employees, you do not have a choice. But, in consulting, aside from a secretary, you may never need anyone else. In today's market with computers and technology, you may not even need a secretary. The client wants you. They are no longer impressed by expensive offices, because they have come to realize that they are paying for it in the long run.

EMPHASIS ON SERVICE

While overhead is kept low, one characteristic that is quite high and always visible in every "failure-proof" enterprise is service. Everyone has heard the term service and knows it is important. But service is more than saying thank you to a customer. It means standing behind a product and/or service; follow-up when the job is done or the merchandise is delivered; dependability in fulfilling promises and meeting delivery dates; and solving problems quickly if any occur.

A problem can mean thousands of dollars in lost time to Walton's customers. He carries a pager and is available during and after working hours. It is not uncommon for him to make a weekend or late night call. Walton understands computer problems can paralyze a company, and he knows that if his response is not rapid, he may lose a client.

He stands behind his work, too. If there is difficulty with an installation, he will return the same day and fix it. He also studies every client's business and industry, and he frequently comes up with money- and time-saving suggestions—a characteristic that has enhanced his value as a service provider.

Walton has proven to his clients that he is not just out to make a quick buck. If they have a computer problem, they can call him anytime, and he will try to solve it for them on the telephone. He never charges for these telephone consultations.

Lana McKendry has the same ethic. She consults with the manufacturers she represents and helps them work out distributor problems. Enormous difficulties can arise in the product business: everything from a distributor not marketing the line to not paying in a timely manner. McKendry has saved several of her manufacturing clients considerable sums of money by passing on information she hears about distributors or home centers.

With Shurcut service is everything. People bring their animals in and they expect them back promptly. One sure way for a groomer to destroy relationships is to keep customers waiting. They expect service—now.

According to Shurcut:

> Grooming is not like buying a loaf of bread or carton of milk. Animal owners know prices will vary, just as the skills of the groomer will. The price a groomer charges is not nearly as sensitive as an everyday item you buy in the store. Pricing and service are the keys. If your customers like the service, they will not hesitate to pay for it. The animal has to come back neat, clean, and well-groomed. They must look good. And, if there is any evidence of mistreatment, you'll never see the owner again. Service, however, always weighs more heavily than the price—unless your fees are outlandish.

Shurcut and Anderson enhance relationships and provide additional service to their clients. They both recommend and sell products that will help customers care for their animals.

Groomers are amateur psychologists, too. They listen patiently when pet owners discuss the habits and idiosyncrasies of their animals. "Most consumers," says Shurcut, "who take the time to have their animal bathed not only care for the dog, but they regard them as part of the family." Smart groomers like Shurcut understand this relationship. It's like a parent/child relationship.

Service is the cornerstone of every "failure-proof" business because in every one of these enterprises, the success of the business is partially due to repeat purchases or buys. Well-run businesses should be able to generate 50 percent or more of their gross from repeat customers.

GENERATING REPEAT BUSINESS

Marketing consultant Jay Abraham, who constantly talks about the failure of businesspeople to follow up with existing clients for that additional order, calls the entire repeat cycle the "marginal net worth" of a customer.

He explains:

> You might spend $100 to get a customer to spend $50 with you for their first purchase, and figure, well, I lost money on that one. But did you? Before saying that you have to do some calculating. Once a customer makes a purchase, how many additional purchases will they make from you during their association? Suppose, for instance, you have that $50 product and/or service. You spend $100 in marketing to draw the customer in the door. Now, suppose your average customer makes three additional purchases. That means your customer is going to spend another $150 before they are finished with

your products. Add that to the $50 they have already spent, and you can see that you will generate $200 from the customer, not $50. That gives you an idea of the importance of repeat business, and providing the service so you get it.

Take Jerry Turner's parking lot striping and repair business. It is five years old and will gross more than $2 million this year. Turner has watched competitors come and go, while his business has grown.

This is a great business and it can be started with an expenditure of less than $10,000. I learned it by working for a striper for several years. I also learned something else that has helped me make it a success. Do not sacrifice quality or service.

When I started in this industry, I worked for a guy and everyone was cutting prices. So was he. Pricing became highly competitive, and in an effort to generate more business, my boss dropped price and cut quality. Never do that. You might get the contract once, but it is doubtful if you will ever see the customer again. My boss never did. In all the time I worked for him, he never had a repeat customer . . . that's what poor quality and inadequate service will do to any business. Today, nearly two-thirds of my customers are repeat.

When you have repeat clients, you don't just earn money on their new jobs, you save money. How? The higher the repeat ratio, the less marketing money you have to spend. Instead of taking out one advertisement after another, small business people who generate high repeat sales find that they do not have to advertise. They get calls from previous customers, and they keep in touch with them via telephone and letters, a much cheaper route than advertising.

Delia Ornaz's maid service generates nearly 90 percent of its business from previous customers. That is an astounding figure considering that Ornaz is in an industry that is overloaded with providers. Still, she has been able to compete successfully and approach an income that is nearly twice that of the average maid service entrepreneur. And she did it with an initial investment of under $1,000.

Few businesses are more sensitive to service than housecleaning. Whether you did a good job or not is immediately visible. Most are never called back. That has never happened to Ornaz. She guarantees her work and "walks through" the residence after the job is finished with the client. If there is a complaint, she immediately redoes the area. She never questions whether the client is right or argues. She says:

> Some of my competitors would cringe at the suggestion of having a walk-through, but I found it is a business-builder. If I am willing to go through a residence, clients believe that I must have done a good job. You also get to know your clientele by walking through the house with them. You establish rapport, keep the client much longer, and generate referrals. This is a phenomenal referral business. Your advertising expenditure is minimal, as is the rest of your overhead.
>
> Many maid services do not do well because they want to get in and out. Some even ask the owner to leave while they clean. That's a marketing mistake. Let the owners stay. Let them see how hard you work for that $50. This is definitely a relationship business.

Bob Levinson runs a relationship business, too. A former advertising agency employee, he carved a niche by providing advertising and public relations services for small enterprises. Most cannot afford the larger agencies, and Levinson filled a definite void. His clients are similar to Tony Walton's, and they share the same concern—they cannot afford to hire a full-time advertising/public relations professional, nor can they afford some of the huge fees that agencies receive. Levinson is a viable alternative.

"To entrepreneurs with a young, struggling business, service is everything. They cannot afford the time to chase vendors. When you make a commitment, you have to live up to it. If you do, you have a client for life," Levinson says. In Levinson's case, he also has a "failure-proof" enterprise that will gross more than $750,000 this year. His start-up capital was less than $10,000, and most of it went for a computer system, fax machine, business telephone, and stationery.

Each of these entrepreneurs has a business with a great many common characteristics. None of their businesses is unusual, and the skills required for their businesses are relatively easy to master. Two of the most important things that have differentiated them from their many competitors are service and experience.

"There are many people out there doing the same thing I do," explains Jerry Turner, "but they may not be conscientious, customer focused, or experienced. Today the entrepreneur who puts service above profit is going to be enormously successful. And he or she has every chance of developing a 'failure-proof' business."

Many small business owners look for the magic formula, a mysterious ingredient that will enable them to open their doors with a product or service that blows everyone away, a product or service that has no competition.

That never happens. It did not happen for any of these "failure-proof" business owners. Each had an enterprise that ran into keen, tough competition. Yet they succeeded thanks to a blend of characteristics ranging from their ability to pick the right business and correct location, to providing superior service with a low overhead—and experience.

But those are not the only characteristics that made these businesses "failure-proof." In the next chapter we take a look at the personal characteristics that each of these "failure-proof" small business owners share.

3

"Failure-Proof"
Business Owners

13 WINNING CHARACTERISTICS

Do failure-proof business owners share common characteristics? Are there behavioral traits that bind them together?
Try these:

- Self-starter
- Risk-taker
- Persistence
- Determining needs
- Analytic ability
- Good management
- Financial expertise
- Self-evaluation
- Marketing ability
- Aggressive
- Proactive
- Service-oriented
- Experienced

SELF-STARTER

Businesspeople who have all of these characteristics are
probably running a "failure-proof" enterprise. Take, for
instance, Jerry Turner, who has been self-employed for 22
years. Here is his assessment of business and what it takes
to run one successfully:

> Nobody is going to kick you in the pants and get
> you moving. You have to be a self-starter. If you're
> not, forget it. When you run your own business, it is
> easy to sit around, waste time, procrastinate, and

avoid the difficult tasks. I learned a long time ago that running your own business is not like working for a corporation. In large companies, if you don't do it, someone else may. But in your own business, if you don't do it, no one will. The buck stops with you.

Mike Goldberg agrees.

Self-starting is a critically important characteristic. I work out of my home, which makes it doubly difficult. There are many temptations within reach— everything from the refrigerator to the television. It's not difficult to sit around and take the easy path. There's no one to push you. To avoid falling into a rut, I set definite weekly goals. I have X amount of calls I must make. I try to take Fridays off, mainly because it is usually a slow day and many other businesspeople are gone by late morning. At the same time, it can also be a great day for making calls because for most businesspeople the telephone is quiet at the end of the week.

I try to put together three-day weekends. That's one of the rewards about owning your own business. You may work your tail off Monday through Thursday, but on Friday you can leave if you've done your job. For me it means making a lot of calls. If I make them, I take off. If not, I work Friday. But there is no one around to jump start me. I must do it by myself.

The inability to be a self-starter can be disastrous. In business, there are numerous unpleasant duties—everything from collecting money to making cold calls, and "failure-proof" business owners have learned they must tackle those unpleasantries first. Then they can go to the easier chores.

"Most positive thinking books stress self-starting," says Goldberg, "because it is one of the most critical characteristics needed in order to succeed. It is easy to sit around, do nothing, and wait for the telephone to ring. In business, you have to make things happen."

RISK-TAKER

Risk-taking is another common characteristic. To leave a salaried, paid position and open your own enterprise in today's economic environment is a risk. Lana McKendry gave up a good-paying job with a future at a home center. She says:

> It took months before I generated any income. There is no question, you have to be willing to take a chance. Nobody wants to fail. It can be devastating, but you have to put yourself on the line. That does not mean you take ridiculous chances. On the contrary, all the risks I've taken have been well thought out beforehand. I knew what I was doing and what the potential could be.

For some "failure-proof" business owners, there was not much choice or significant risk. Tony Walton was out of work and knew his unemployment benefits would not last forever. Delia Ornaz knew she could always go back to work for the maid service if her efforts to start her own business failed. Kendall Shurcut could continue to work for minimum wages at the pet store, or take a chance at opening his own grooming shop. In most cases the risk was lessened because of the relatively low investment. Risking $5,000 to start a consulting practice or an advertising agency is not as chancy and nerve-wracking as putting up $250,000 to open a restaurant. Most important, each risk-taker knew the business and the potential return.

Chase Revel, founder of *Entrepreneur* Magazine says, "Don't ever think that small business is risk-free. It isn't. There is no sure thing, but there is no sure thing in anything. Even if you work for someone, you can be laid off or fired at any time. Running your own small business does not have any greater risk."

THE PERSISTENCE FACTOR

Self-starting, risk-taking. They are both important to the success of a business, but equally as important is persistence. Entrepreneurs who retreat when they are turned down, or if they run into difficulties, will not succeed. Or at least they will never create a "failure-proof" enterprise. None of the "failure-proof" business owners we discuss lacked persistence. It is one of their most common traits.

Mike Goldberg called publishers over and over again in order to get them to listen to his proposal to represent their magazines.

"Persistence ranks up there with self-starting," he says, "insofar as survival in the business. You get on the telephone in the morning, and it is easy to throw in the towel when you hear the first no."

Goldberg endures countless nos when he is selling ads for his clients or trying to convince publishers to let him handle their accounts. His day is filled with negatives. Still, he knows the importance of pursuing his daily objectives.

Jerry Turner gets almost as many nos as Mike. He has been in the parking lot striping and paving business for more than five years, and he has had his share of nos. He explains:

Many of the purchasing agents I meet or have dealt with are used to dealing with certain people. It is difficult to get them to switch, or to even give you a chance. It takes persistence, and understanding that when someone turns you down there is nothing personal about it.

If they have a vendor, there is always the chance something will happen and they may want to change. If I quit asking, they would simply find someone else. If you are always there, you stand a chance of getting the job if something happens or if it is put out to bid. That does not mean you should be a pest. Persistence means sticking to it, but do not bug prospects to death. Do it in a planned, timely basis: when the lot is due for striping or the business is put out to bid. Just be there.

Jay Horoki gave up a potentially promising accounting career to clean buildings. Initially most of the people he talked to dealt with a janitorial service and did not want to switch. "The inability to change is a human characteristic that haunts you in business. People may have a vendor who is not doing a good job, but they still will not switch. They like the status quo. You've just got to be there—all the time. When the moment comes when they do switch, you're in line."

The epitome of persistence is Arnold Van Den Berg, an immigrant who came to the United States after World War II, barely graduated high school, became an auto mechanic for a brief time, and suddenly decided to pursue his lifelong dream to become a money manager. He did, and today he is one of the most successful in the country, handling port-folios that are approaching $100 million.

But it was not easy. When it happened it was almost a "revelation." Van Den Berg had graduated high school and found a job as a mechanic. One day, he recalls, it suddenly occurred to him that he would spend the next 50 years of his life doing the same thing. Did he want to spend his life under a car? No.

Van Den Berg wanted to be a money manager—an investment counselor who makes money not by trading in stocks and bonds but rather on the success of the portfolios he handles. If he invests wisely and shows an excellent return for his clients, he shares a percentage of those returns. If he does not, he usually finds himself looking for other clients.

Becoming a money manager is not easy, especially if you have only a high school education. Still, Van Den Berg was determined. He studied money and finance and read every book on the topic he could find. Slowly his knowledge grew, and with it his eagerness to get into the business.

The opportunity came when he met two other young men who wanted to enter the field. They were college educated, astute, and glib. Van Den Berg was confident that they knew what they were talking about. When they offered to make him a partner, he jumped. All three entered the fray together.

What happened next is something Van Den Berg does not recall with a smile. They opened a firm, clients began to come through the door, money was invested, and then, almost overnight, the investments soured and the two college-educated partners disappeared.

Although nothing illegal had transpired, Van Den Berg felt an obligation to those who had put their money into his hands. For the next three years he lived and worked out of one-bedroom apartment/office. He sold insurance and did anything he could to raise money to pay his investors back. Finally, after more than three years, he paid off the debt.

One investor was so impressed with Van Den Berg's honesty that he decided to give him another chance. The client gave him $10,000 to invest. Van Den Berg did, and the rest, as they say, is history. Van Den Berg's business grew along with his reputation. By the late 1980s he had one of the most successful money management firms in the country.

He credits his success to

> ... persistence, and the fact I was not going to let one disappointment discourage me. Since that time I have studied entrepreneurs and the characteristics that make them successful. Invariably, if you look at a person who has done well, the characteristic that stands out is persistence—the ability to stick to it when everything else seems lost.

Kendall Shurcut agrees. When he opened his grooming parlor, customers did not flock into his shop. He says:

> It took time. I had to win them over and convince them I would do a good job. People are not prone to switch vendors easily. I had to win them over and convince them I would do a good job. The only way you do that is by example. You give the best service possible. In today's market, service is something everyone wants, but few people give. If you provide it, you can build a tremendous business.

Shurcut did.

> Eventually, after I got one or two people to try my shop, the business started to build. Business is not for the faint of heart. There are times you feel like quitting, but you must persist. I thought about things I could do if I wasn't grooming. There wasn't anything open. Where could a guy without a college education, someone who just made passing grades in high school, go to find a good job? Grooming was it. It was my chance to do my own thing. If you stick

with it and have some of the other entrepreneurial characteristics, you will succeed.

Bob Levinson says

I think you have to have a desire to do your own thing. You also have to feel that you do not need a weekly paycheck. You're willing to take a chance, put everything you have into it, and not be afraid of going broke. If you think too much about the money, you're going to fail, because that's all that occupies your mind. You should be thinking of getting and servicing clients, not collecting money.

Although all successful "failure-proof" business owners are persistent, that does not mean they do not know when to quit. "If you start an enterprise and it just does not work out, get out," says Revel. "Most of us do not want to admit we made a mistake. We try to hang on. Sometimes we hang on too long. You have to use common sense. Is the business going to make it? Can it?"

To make that call, businesspeople have to be able to analyze what they are doing and evaluate the market objectively. Most businesses do not make money from the day they open; however, within a reasonable amount of time, they should. How reasonable? "Check your capital," Revel says with a smile. "How long can you hold out? Is the business building? Are you reaching more prospects? That's a call only a business owner can make, but it should be made. Don't go on just for the sake of owning your own shop."

DETERMINING NEEDS

The future—if there is one—of any business is determined by the owner's ability to determine the needs of the audience, to think as they do. "Put yourself in your customers' shoes," advises Revel. "Envision their needs. Does your product or service answer them?"

Every successful "failure-proof" business owner is adept at determining needs. Shurcut explains:

> For example, in my business I am not just bathing dogs to get them clean. I'm dealing with one of the most important possessions a person has and the need they have is to (1) have their animal look and smell clean and (2) have the animal treated kindly and come out with a minimum of trauma. You may be the best groomer in town, but if the animals you deal with come out traumatized, chances are the owner will never be back. You have to deal with the animal *and* the owner.

Understanding needs means entrepreneurs should have the ability to empathize with customers. Says McKendry:

> In my business, I found the buyers are just as interested in service as merchandise. They not only worry about stock being in the store on time, but they are also concerned about the display and how it looks. Anyone who is a rep in this field and tries to make it strictly on the basis of a quality product will miss. You cannot forget the service part of the enterprise. You have to be able to read the customers.

Mike Goldberg agrees.

> I have two customers I must empathize with. One is the magazine publisher, who wants you to sell ads and generate money. When I do that, I am an extension of their publication. A representative. They want to feel comfortable that I will leave a

positive impression on every prospect I talk to. They don't just want the ad revenue, they want me to help build an image for the publication, as well.

My second customer is the advertiser. They want me to take care of everything once the sale is made. They rely upon me to get them good placement and to let them know when the deadline is near. You don't just sell and run. Everything in this business is service. The more service you provide, the greater success you are going to have as a rep. Forget service, and you won't last long.

The ability to read customers is critical, says Jerry Turner. Parking lot owners want him to do a good job.

But they also want a minimum of inconvenience to their customers. If I say I am going to be finished by a certain day or time I'd better do it, because regardless of how good a job I do, I've blown it if I inconvenience the store.

Some stripers enter the business and have problems right from the start. Those difficulties usually stem from the fact they do not read the customer. They may be striping and doing the lot at 11 A.M. on a weekday, just when the store's customers are arriving. You have to be aware that striping is not the prime business of the person who hires you. They sell merchandise, and they do not want you interfering with the flow of their customers. Become a hindrance, and you lose a contract.

ANALYTIC ABILITY

Listening and analyzing skills are critical characteristics for consultants such as Dennis McCuistion.

Clients tell you what they want, but they frequently do not say what they need. A bank may call me in to determine why a certain department has not been functioning correctly, but they want more than that. They want me to give them a plan to change the department so it will operate smoothly.

Consultants are aware that when they are called in the client usually knows what's wrong. What they need is a remedy. That's what they pay you for, and a consultant has to realize that's the reason behind the call.

"Failure-proof" consultants can recognize mixed signals from prospective clients, too. "The president of the firm will tell you he wants one thing, and the managers tell you something entirely different. You have to carefully listen to each side before you can discern what is needed," says McCuistion.

"If you're unable to determine the customer's needs," says Revel, "you are not going to make it."

MANAGEMENT ABILITY

"Failure-proof" businesspeople share another characteristic: management ability. There are stories galore about entrepreneurs who start a business, develop it, and then go by the wayside because they were poor managers.

The owners/managers of "failure-proof" businesses are composites of many desirable managerial characteristics, and each is as important as the other. Good managers must be able to deal with customers, but they also have to be able to handle suppliers.

Kendall Shurcut spends time talking and relating to dog owners, but he has to be able to deal with suppliers of the shampoo he uses. If he does not have good supplier relationships, he could run out of shampoo in the middle of a busy season.

Shurcut has to be able to schedule. How many dogs can he bathe in a day? How many big ones? Small ones? How far apart should he schedule them? How much help will he need? What about the shampoo; will he have enough on hand for the following week? How does he know? How far in advance should he order shampoo? How long does it take to get it?

Each of those questions may sound relatively simple, but the answers determine whether Shurcut is a success or a failure. How much should he charge each patron? Can he calculate the correct fees, based on the size of the animal and how long he thinks the grooming will take?

What should he do to market to his customers? What about getting new customers; how does he generate them? What if he runs short of working capital; what should he do? What kind of insurance does he need for his coworkers and the animals? What is his liability?

Despite the myriad abilities of many entrepreneurs, not many can do everything, from sales and service to accounting. They need help, and that means hiring a part-timer or going to an outside service. Regardless of which path the owners goes, it takes management ability.

Lana McKendry has never taken a management course, but she can handle her business, which did more than $20 million in sales last year. McKendry's management duties include dealing with her manufacturing clients, home center buyers, and suppliers who provide her with materials and displays for the center. She must understand manufacturing lead time—for both the product and the display fabricator—and be able to balance payments so she can pay for displays and product.

Managers have another audience aside from customers—their employees. Unlike large corporations, in a small business environment everyone knows each other. Employees know the owner, and they are not isolated from him or her as they would be from the president of a major corporation.

The personality of the manager/owner has an enormous impact on employees. If the owner is in a bad mood, depressed, or angry, it spreads through the workplace quickly. Poor attitudes can kill a business even though the product and/or service is superior. A few years ago an aggressive manufacturer opened a small retail store in Beverly Hills, where he sold a variety of imported jewelry at bargain prices.

The jewelry was high quality, and before long word had spread about the superior merchandise. The businessman's revenue doubled, tripled, and quadrupled within months. He was sitting on a gold mine—and then it collapsed as the holiday season approached. The orders came in heavier, and everyone, from those on the manufacturing line to the shipping facility, was under pressure to get the goods out. They did, but in many cases the merchandise was flawed. Complaints came in and a customer service department was put under stress, as well.

As the holidays neared, the organization became more disorganized than ever. The owner did little to help. His skills were confined to marketing and coming up with innovative new jewelry designs. He could see various departments getting into more trouble as each day passed. What did he do? He yelled and screamed. He threatened. The more he lost his temper, the worse the company seemed to be. By the time the holidays were over, half his employees had quit, customers were howling, and his manufacturing line had collapsed. In the end, he refunded nearly half of the revenue he collected, and the business almost collapsed.

A good manager is able to juggle many different hats at the same time. Business owners need that know-how, and if they do not have it, they must hire someone who does. Wearing different hats takes skill and the understanding that you must deal with a variety of customers (employees, suppliers, and customers) on a daily basis.

FINANCIAL EXPERTISE

Marketing acumen is, of course, critical to the success of any enterprise, but so is financial ability. It is a characteristic that frequently makes the difference between success and failure. Regardless of one's ability to generate sales and deal with employees, management's lack of financial expertise could be a death blow to the enterprise.

Financial expertise means more than tracking dollars and cents. It means setting priorities insofar as where the company is going to spend its monies and when. There is no need, for example, to have fancy, expensive offices if clients never visit. A mail order enterprise can operate out of a garage; a manufacturing facility, in a reasonably priced industrial park; a consultant or a computer repair specialist, from the home.

A trademark of "failure-proof" entrepreneurs has been their ability to watch the dollars. Astute business owners constantly ask, "Will this expenditure impact my business positively, or is it just for my pleasure?" Is it necessary for the groomer to buy a new Mercedes?

Needless expenditures can backfire. The customer may look at the new car, high-rent office, and expensive furniture and theorize that the reason the person's fees are so high is to cover overhead.

Consider this example. A group of financial consultants rented the penthouse and the floor below it of a newly constructed high-rise office building. They spent several hundred thousand dollars in renovations and installed solid wood staircases between both floors. Imported desks were brought in along with other expensive furnishings and rugs.

A grand opening party, costing more than $30,000, heralded the arrival of the new company. Everyone, including the mayor, local civic and community groups, and professional organizations, was on hand for the opening. The only thing missing were clients. Few came, and those who did were worried that their investment funds would be going toward the consultants' extravagant lifestyle.

Within six months the young company was running out of capital. By the ninth month, they had renegotiated the lease and given up one floor. By year's end, they closed the doors. Contrast this with the lifestyle of Arnold Van Den Berg, one of the "failure-proof" financial entrepreneurs, who originally operated out of his apartment bedroom. When he had enough capital, he moved into a modest office that had room for a library, reception area, and two additional offices. Van Den Berg occasionally had clients visit, but none ever complained about the modest but tasteful lifestyle. They knew their money was being invested just as wisely. Expensive cars and suites may be fine for doctors and lawyers, but are they really needed for most businesses in today's volatile economy?

Start-up business owners must be able to crawl before they walk. Every dollar saved is a dollar profit. Revel, who has operated out of everything from a P.O. box to luxury offices, says the question that must be asked is "If I spend this cash for that particular piece of goods (or services), will it return a profit to me and my business? A simple, important question. If not, invest in something else, or save the funds for working capital."

SELF-EVALUATION

"Failure-proof" business owners are astute when it comes to allocating their capital, and they have common sense and objectivity when it comes to analyzing their abilities.

Small business people do not let ego get in the way of judgment either. The choices can be tough, but if it means laying someone off or keeping the person and going into debt, there is no doubt as to the decision. Good small business operators are like generals. They lead the troops and make tough decisions when necessary. No one feels good about laying off employees, but it may have to be done.

"I don't like to fire anyone," says Turner, "but if your business dips, it can be a matter of survival." Revel agrees. "You can't keep people if you do not need them. They may have families, but so do you. We had to face layoffs several times at *Entrepreneur*. It doesn't make you feel good, but it has to be done."

MARKETING ABILITY

Marketing is another characteristic that many "failure-proof" business owners have mastered. A better mousetrap does not mean people will beat a path to your door. Customers have to know about it, and getting the news out requires advertising, public relations, merchandising, promotion, and other marketing-oriented skills. If the entrepreneur does not have the marketing skills, he or she must hire someone—freelance, part time, or full time—who does.

Networking is part of the marketing mix. Shurcut goes to trade shows where he not only meets pet product manufacturers, but other groomers, who may be in a position to recommend clients they know are moving into his area.

Lana McKendry travels to major hardware and home shows, where she meets manufacturers and home center buyers. She goes to countless cocktail parties and receptions at the shows and, admittedly, is "tired of them" but must go.

Mike Goldberg can be found at many national pet trade shows, where he meets both potential advertisers and the managers/owners of other pet-oriented trade magazines who may have booths at the show.

Consultants get involved in local community groups and organizations, and they try to maintain a visible profile. Joining just to join does not work. They must actively participate.

All business owners examine their audience/market and determine what organizations they should join, which events they should attend, and how often should they be there. They write letters, spend time on the telephone, and read trade papers in addition to local and national newspapers so they know what is going on in their industry.

The Need to be Aggressive

Being aggressive is a characteristic that every successful entrepreneur shares. It relates closely to persistence, however, there is a small but important distinction. "Persistence," says McKendry, "is to keep pounding away at accounts and not giving up. Being aggressive is to go out there and find the accounts so you have someone to 'keep pounding away at.' "

To Shurcut, it means "you cannot sit back and wait for business to come in the door. Certainly, you are going to get a number of referrals, but you always have to be looking and pursuing new prospects. It is as simple as carrying business cards and giving them to people you happen to meet. It means making sure that everyone you come in contact with knows you are in business and what business you are in . . . that's aggressive."

The Proactive Entrepreneur

Too many businesspeople are reactive. That is, something happens and they react to it instead of anticipating and planning for the event or change.

The emergence of huge discount centers such as the Price Club and Home Depot took advantage of the consumer's desire for one-stop convenient shopping and better pricing. Smaller hardware and do-it-yourself stores watched in amazement as their business disappeared into the huge marts. Today, the neighborhood hardware store has become a dinosaur, with many owners simply shuttering their doors because they were unable to see the trend. They were reactive, not proactive.

Consultant Tony Walton saw downsizing and cutbacks and realized the cutbacks would create an opening for his computer service enterprise. Dennis McCuistion watched as banks and savings and loans did the same thing, and he knew there would be a need for someone with his financial expertise.

Most successful entrepreneurs are proactive. They have the ability to see ahead; to determine what is going to happen, where the voids will be—and they fill them.

Communicative Ability

Communication is a characteristic that is absolutely necessary if a businessperson is to become successful. The manufacturer's rep who fails to communicate why a certain item is not being stocked, will fare no better than the dog groomer who neglects to tell a customer why they changed the grooming instructions.

Customers want to be kept informed, and small businesspeople look upon communication as an ability that is just as important as the job itself.

When Jay Horoki·started his janitorial service, he made sure that he sat down with every client and explained exactly how his crew was going to operate. Delia Ornaz did the same with her maid service, and Dennis McCuistion does the same with his banking clients.

Service Oriented

Take care of the customer. If there is one characteristic that every failure-proof business exhibits it is service. Nothing is left to chance. Jerry Turner's former boss never gave proper service to his clients. As a result, there were never any referrals, and the business never prospered. Kendall Shurcut goes out of his way to ensure that the animals his clients bring in are not only well-groomed, but they are taken care of until the customer comes to pick them up.

Every successful small business owner realizes one thing—bad word of mouth is easy to come by and hard to shake. While positive customers can help a business, negative ones can ruin it.

The Experience Factor

Perhaps one of the keys to success is experience. Know the business and industry. All of the entrepreneurs in this book had experience in their field before they launched their own enterprise. Knowing the industry gave them an edge. They knew what to expect and they were familiar with problems that businesspeople in their field frequently encountered. Knowing those problems in advance gave them the chance to not only prepare for them, but find solutions as well.

Shurcut worked in a grooming shop; Ornaz toiled as a maid for others before she started her own company;

McCuistion worked in the banking/financial field before opening his doors; Walton spent his early career in the computer area; Goldberg sold for a plethora of magazines and dealt with numerous advertising accounts. They all knew their industry, and although that knowledge did not guarantee success, it certainly helped.

Creating a business that becomes "failure-proof" takes work. It requires the characteristics and traits that have been outlined. "Failure-proof" business owners display these features constantly. But what about prospective small business owners, entrepreneurs who would like to establish a successful small business? Is there some technique they can apply, come test they can take that will indicate their chances for success?

Although there is no definitive test to determine the absolute failure or success chances of a prospective businessperson, the answers to certain questions will give an indication of how entrepreneurial a person happens to be.

THE BUSINESSPERSON CHARACTERISTIC EQUATION

This quiz, which does not have a pass/fail score, was put together with the assistance of several psychologists at a California university. Assign 3 points (total) to each answer. You can give all 3 to any one of the two activities; you can give 2 to one and 1 to the other or you can split the three points between the two activities.

1. I would rather:
   a. Be the leader of the band _____
   b. Play one of the lead instruments _____

2. I would rather:

a. Design a game and the rules _____

b. Play and win the game _____

3. I would rather:

a. Sell something to someone _____

b. Work on a spreadsheet analysis _____

4. I would rather:

a. Carry out the marketing plan _____

b. Design the marketing plan _____

5. I would rather:

a. Run my own business _____

b. Be president of a major corporation _____

6. I would rather:

a. Buy a proven franchise and run it _____

b. Start my own business and run it _____

7. I would rather:

a. Create businesses in my mind_____

b. Daydream about new ideas _____

8. I would rather:

a. Balance the checkbook _____

b. Help others solve their problems _____

9. I would rather:

a. Listen to others _____

b. Have others listen to me _____

10. I would rather:

a. Ask questions of others _____

b. Have others question me _____

Part II
Preference Test

For this next series, score 0–3 points for each answer.

If, for instance, you never served as an elected official, score 0. If you have, score 3. With other questions score according to preference, with 3 (highest) if you enjoy that activity to the fullest, and 1 or 2 if you only moderately enjoy it.

11. I have served as an elected official in high school or college.

12. I have won an award as a salesperson.

13. I am a good salesperson.

14. I like to plan entertainment for a party.

15. I don't mind going someplace alone.

16. I like working in an office.

17. I have organized a group or club.

18. I have had my own business.

19. I know how to be a leader.

20. I keep accurate records of bills, payments, and sales.

The first ten questions indicate the type activities you prefer and your attitude toward leadership. Leadership is one of the indicators as to how successful you may be in business. The greater your leadership score, the more likely you are to fit into your own business. In your own enterprise, you have to be a leader and make the decisions.

The activities that are the highest indicators of leadership are 1a, 2a, 3a, 4b, 5a, 6b, 7a, 8b, 9b, and 10a.

In Question 1, it's obvious which answer carries the most leadership "points." Question 2 is a bit more subtle, as you must choose between "design" and "win." Both, of course, are desirable entrepreneurial characteristics, but designing a game and its rules shows that the person wants to be the force behind the event. That's the way leaders think.

Question 3 is not much of a mystery either. Selling something is more of a leadership trait than working on a spreadsheet. In Question 4, designing a marketing plan shows more leadership than carrying one out.

In Question 5, running your own business is more entrepreneurial than being president of a major corporation. Presidents have to answer to board of directors, whereas most small business owners answer to no one but themselves (and possibly the banker).

In Question 6, starting your own business is more difficult than buying a franchise. Franchisees have complete instructions and guidelines. With a franchise it is hard to miss, but you may have no guidelines to follow when starting your own business. It is definitely more difficult, challenging, and identified with entrepreneurs.

Question 7 is interesting and both answers are close in value. Most entrepreneurs like to create something in their minds. They are always thinking of new businesses, products, and services and how they might introduce it to the market. But daydreaming about new ideas is not totally without leadership and entrepreneurial connotations. Entrepreneurs do daydream about ideas.

Question 8 is relatively straightforward. Solving a problem—which is what small business owners face daily—is more entrepreneurial and contains more leadership qualities than balancing the checkbook.

Question 9 dwells on one critical characteristic that every entrepreneur must have—listening ability. Having others listen only proves that the person doing the talking has a large ego. It does not tell you anything about the potential business skills. This question should have points scored in each answer.

The same is true for question 10. Entrepreneurs are curious and want to know why things are as they are. They want to know why some audiences will buy a product while others will not. They like to ask questions. That's how "failure-proof" business owners test market products and services.

If you scored 30 points (three for each) in these categories, you undoubtedly have leadership ability and would probably make a "failure-proof" small business entrepreneur. If you scored less, that does not mean you are a B or C student. It simply implies that you do not have as strong a set of small business characteristics as someone else who may be fixated on opening a business.

Part II questions offer a similar indicator. Scoring 24 (3 points for each except for questions 16 and 20) means you may be perfect for starting your own business. Most of these questions (save 16 and 20) are preferences that indicate you obviously like entrepreneurial activities.

For example, question 15 may not seem to indicate an entrepreneurial preference, but it does. Entrepreneurs often have to face things and start an enterprise without support. They do it alone. Therefore, "going someplace alone" is something that is not at all unpleasant.

Question 16 (working in an office) and 20 (keeping accurate records) are activities that every entrepreneur has to do to run a business. They are, of course, the least glamorous activities, but they still are important.

Preferences are important although not definitive. Your score is not the final word as to whether you will be successful or not. It is, however, an indicator as to how strong your entrepreneurial characteristics happen to be.

In the next chapter we look at some of the "failure-proof" businesses to which those entrepreneurial characteristics can be applied.

4

Successful Businesses and Their Owners

You do not need millions of dollars in order to make millions. Every "failure-proof" business in this book was developed with an investment of less than $10,000. Some were launched for under $5,000, and most for less than $1,000.

None of the businesses is a revolutionary concept, either. Chase Revel sold advice through *Entrepreneur*, much the same as any other consultant, only he did it via a newsletter.

In a recent issue of *Inc.* Magazine, author James C. Collins points out that "a surprising number of companies we consider great today did not start out with a compelling idea for a product or service. . . ." Collins goes on to write that too many potential entrepreneurs believe they have to come up with a startling, innovative concept in order to be successful. That is not true. In fact, the founders of such companies as Sony, Hewlett-Packard, Marriott, Motorola, Honda, Disney, Wal-Mart, and Nordstroms did not open their doors with anything that would be considered a "great idea."

How, then, did they become so successful? How do "failure-proof" businesses emerge if the concept is not original?

For the most part, entrepreneurs who do well are excellent managers and have a clear vision of what they want to do. If they enter a competitive industry, they examine how others are doing business before they open their doors. Most of the time they find a way to do it differently and better. They do not need original ideas. They execute.

Entrepreneurs are aware of the economy and the impact it has had on business. Thus during the past few years there has been a tremendous rise in the number of consultants to replace the many workers who have been laid off or had their positions outsourced. Astute entrepreneurs also can see into the future, and they can easily forecast that the need for consultants will grow, as will the demand for those offering personal services. They also can see that services often considered mundane offer an excellent opportunity for successful businesses, and they tailor-make their "failure-proof" enterprises to take advantage of areas of growing need. We will now look in greater detail at a number of the most successful small businesses in the United States.

COMPUTERIZED JANITORIAL SERVICES

Janitorial work goes back hundreds of years. There is nothing revolutionary about it, but it can be one of the most profitable small businesses in the country—particularly when technology is blended into the business. Although the field is competitive, there is opportunity for those who want to enter it.

Typically, janitors work through landlords (owners) of building and office complexes. In most cases large complexes hire a service to clean the buildings on a regular basis. The cleaning fee becomes part of the tenant's rent, and the person and/or company that rents the space has little say.

But an enormous number of small and medium-size office buildings and industrial complexes do not incorporate cleaning into their agreements. It is up to individual tenants to retain their own janitor and set the rules. This is the area that is full of opportunity.

In most small and medium-size offices, the janitorial contract is given to the first janitor through the door after the office manager moves in, someone the office manager or owner knows from previous cleaning, or someone the landlord/building owner knows.

Difficult business to break into? Not really. Ask Jay Horoki.

From the day he began working, the business fascinated him. He recognized that it lent itself to computerization, yet his company and most of the others he knew of in the industry were not using computers.

Each night his crew cleaned the same complex, and in the months he supervised he never heard a word from the owner, positive *or* negative. Each office was cleaned the same as the next. In three months Horoki never received a message from a landlord or tenant that something was missed or that some special service would be needed. Nor did Horoki's employer, the owner of the janitorial service, have any special follow-up procedures. He seldom communicated with clients, nor did he track the cleaning, the amount of time it took to do it, or which crews were more efficient.

Horoki was fascinated by the opportunity. When he opened his own service, he targeted small and midsize complexes. Once he generated an agreement, he walked through the offices with the manager and determined exactly what was needed and what areas were most important. Did anything require special treatment? Horoki put his findings and a client's history and remarks on computer.

When a cleaning crew went to work, each crew's supervisor was provided with a computer printout and a sheet to fill out. The sheet contained each client's specific requirements, and the supervisors had to go through each, check the work off, and put in the time it was completed.

Horoki took these findings and generated monthly reports with comments that were sent to clients. Few of his competitors did anything like this. They would walk through, make mental notes or scribble on a scratch pad, but they were not as thorough as Horoki. Nor did they think about follow-up with the client, a concept that Horoki not only learned in business school but understood was critical to the well-being of any service business. "You do not just provide the service and forget it," says Horoki. "In today's business environment, every service business has to follow-up. If you leave the client and never communicate with them, you stand a good chance of being knocked off by a competitor who is more communicative."

Absentee Ownership—Does It Work?

Horoki was not an absentee business owner relying on the supervisors in his crew to provide him with data. In fact, not one of the "failure-proof" enterprises detailed in this book is run by an absentee owner. To be successful, owners have to be involved and around.

Horoki made unannounced, surprise visits, inspecting areas to make sure they were cleaned the way the tenant expected. The visits not only ensured that the job was being done, but it kept his supervisors on their toes and guaranteed that their nightly reports were accurate.

Horoki says:

> You don't act like a spy, but a concerned business owner. I wanted to know if any of my people were having difficulties. Were their assignments too much to cover in an evening? Was there some part of the job that was becoming difficult to the point where I had to ask for a higher cleaning fee? Regardless of how smooth your business seems to be running, never turn into an absentee owner. That's one path that can lead to problems.

SOLVING EMPLOYEE TURNOVER

The janitorial business has high employee turnover, primarily because of the low pay scale and lack of benefits. This turnover caused wasted time and additional expense when an employee left. Even though janitorial workers are not high on the pay scale and replacing them was not difficult, training workers took time. That meant lost revenue.

"Turnover means lost time and money for every business," cautions Horoki. "Turnover can hurt this business more from a profitability standpoint than almost anything else."

Horoki tried to eliminate turnover. While most janitorial crews rely on part-timers or even transients, Horoki hired full-time workers, trained them, paid them a premium wage, and put regular review processes into play. He says:

> Small businesses do many things better than large companies, but one thing we can all learn from major corporations is the importance of training to make workers more productive. It enables them to perform better, and helps them realize they are part of a team and company. If it is done correctly, the employee begins to see that this job is not just a temporary stop.

Horoki introduced benefits into the pay package. His idea was to keep the same crew and develop it into a dedicated group of workers. It took time, but the training and emphasis on professionalism worked.

In two years Horoki never lost a client. This success is not surprising. The government ranks janitorial (and maid) service as two of the fastest-growing industries in the country. Janitorial services are not unique, nor are they a great, new idea, but they are highly profitable, rewarding service businesses . . . when run correctly and efficiently.

Businesses do not have to be unusual or glamorous to be profitable. Not everyone is going to come up with a new light bulb, or an electronic chip that revolutionizes computers, but for the entrepreneur who is persistent and develops a new wrinkle with an old product or service, there is just as much potential for profitability.

SIMPLE IDEAS MAKE MONEY

James Collins, author of *Beyond Entrepreneurship: Turning Your Business into an Enduring Great Company*, cites examples of other well-known entrepreneurs who lacked great ideas but did not lack in their dedication and marketing skills: everyone from Sam Walton and J. Willard Marriott to Procter & Gamble. None had revolutionary ideas, just revolutionary leaders who offered many familiar products in a "new, service-oriented package." For the most part, that's what makes a failure-proof business.

THE PUBLISHING REP

A publisher's representative is not unique enterprise, either. But, like Marriott and Walton, Mike Goldberg took a concept, improved it, and developed a winning enterprise. Goldberg's idea can be adapted to a number of industries, and the business will continue to grow because of today's economic conditions.

Downsizing has hit the publishing industry, too. Additionally, there is tremendous competition for advertising dollars. Magazines compete not only with other publications in the same industry, but they also have the added chore of battling television, newspapers, and radio, plus the emerging cable stations and new publications that pop up daily.

Publishers' representatives operate in one of two ways. They can work exclusively for one magazine and earn a paycheck plus a commission on the advertisements they sell, or they can represent a collection of magazines as an independent rep. If they choose the latter path, they work on their own and get a commission when they sell an ad. There is no salary or fringe benefits, but there can be a draw against sales.

Independent reps who work for more than one magazine usually avoid conflicts by handling only one magazine per industry. Why? Say an independent rep who works for both *Time* and *Newsweek* sold space to automobile manufacturers or insurance companies for both magazines. If she gets an insertion order for Buick, for example, and it only covers one magazine, which magazine would she recommend?

To avoid conflicts, many reps represent only one magazine per industry or trade. (Every industry belongs to a trade. For instance, automotive is a trade, so is insurance, pets, food, restaurants. And every industry has so-called trade publications that are distributed only to those within the trade—to insurance salespeople in the insurance industry; restaurant owners in the restaurant field.) Thus, a rep might represent one newsmagazine that might cater to auto enthusiasts (or the auto trade), perhaps one that was distributed in the retail trade, and one that went to those involved in the computer industry (another trade publication).

A rep could sell advertising space in automotive, food, or electronic magazines—three different trades representing three different industries. This system breeds inefficiency, however, because reps have to have in-depth knowledge about three or four different industries. They have to be an authority on each. That takes time, study, and education. Because industries change all the time, reps must spend almost as many hours keeping up as they do selling advertisements.

Goldberg knew the process and felt that reps had to know too much. They wasted time. Instead of picking out three or four industries and selling ads for publications in those fields, he came up with a new approach. He studied the business and was convinced there were numerous magazines—in the same industry—that were noncompetitive.

Goldberg explains:

There was no reason why a rep could not handle a half dozen (or more) of these publications in the same industry, as long as they all reached a different audience and were noncompetitive when it came to the advertisers.

There could be an advertiser who might buy space in more than one, but they would be looking for a different audience. For instance, within the same industry you oftentimes find a trade that caters to distributors, while another is targeted at the retailer, while a third can be geared toward consumers.

An advertiser might be interested in reaching both audiences. If so, they could purchase an ad in each—and if I represented all three magazines, I would receive a commission on each. A second advantage would be that in one meeting, I could sell an advertiser two or three ads—all to the same industry, but in a different publication with a different audience. It would be a timesaver for me.

Goldberg started with the pet industry. If, for instance, he sold space in a bird magazine, he would not take on a competing bird magazine. Instead, he would sell space in a dog or cat magazine or a boarding kennel publication. None competed against each other, but all had common advertisers. "The magazine business is tough, but the pet industry is healthy, which means there is a great opportunity to sell ads. Don't pick a loser—like automobiles."

Goldberg did something else, too. While most reps sold in a local or regional area, he convinced his client publications that he could be productive and solicit advertisements across the country, on a national basis. It was intriguing for the magazines, because they did not have to seek a different rep in every major metropolitan area. Goldberg offered them convenience. With one telephone call they could reach him and determine how he was doing.

The risk was minimal for publishers. They signed an agreement appointing Goldberg their rep, but it had a 30-day cancellation clause. They could get rid of him at any time if he did not produce.

"I picked an industry I knew. Even though all magazines are in a profit squeeze, the pet industry is not only growing rapidly, it is also relatively recession proof, which meant I could continue to make a living even if the economy took an occasional dip."

Goldberg's income—after one year—was in the six-figure range. His total investment was under $2,000 for telephone equipment, fax machine, and a computer system to track clients and provide an accounting and word processing capability. He kept his office rent minimal, too, by working out of his apartment.

"The people you work for do not care what your office looks like because they never visit. They only care about results. In the two years I have been an independent rep, I have never had a client come to my office, and I doubt it will ever happen."

MOBILE DOG GROOMING

While downsizing and outsourcing have been the major impetus behind the emergence of numerous businesses, two other needs—to save time and to shop conveniently—have become the reason behind the rise of a number of enterprises.

Time and convenience factors have driven the emergence of a host of successful enterprises, including convenience stores, home shopping on television, catalog/mail order products, fast-food restaurants, and the rising tide of home delivery for products ranging from pizza and chicken to cleaning.

Time and convenience are two of the reasons for the success of a 25-year-old enterprise that has suddenly become a booming business—mobile dog grooming. Aside from being in one of the country's fastest and steadiest growth industries (pets), mobile grooming offers an opportunity to the unskilled worker.

The heaviest concentrations of mobile groomers are in Florida and California, where there are huge numbers of retirees who prefer to have someone else bathe their animals and the weather is conducive to year-round business. Mobile groomers (groomers bathe and groom the dog/cat) also are found in states with four seasons, and many of them have year-round clients since bathing and grooming can be a 12-month business. Shurcut and Anderson, for instance, have educated and conditioned their customers. The clients know it is important to groom an animal year-round, not just during flea season. Still, in areas where it is relatively warm all-year round, business is usually better. There is no "season" for the business, but mobile groomers are definitely busier in summer than winter.

Mobile groomers offer a simple benefit to customers. While people could drive to the local grooming parlor, many opt for the convenience of the mobile groomer—an entrepreneur who comes to your door and bathes your animal in a specially-equipped van parked in the driveway.

Aside from convenience, customers like the mobile approach because they do not have to take their animals away from the home environment to a groomer's storefront. The animal remains in the friendly confines of the home—the driveway. There is less trauma, which is an important consideration for animal owners, especially those who spend the time and money to have their animals bathed and groomed.

The business has several advantages for the groomer,

too. It has low overhead—no storefront rent to be paid—
and minimal advertising costs, since most business is generated via referral and the sign on the groomer's truck.
There's another advantage—mobile groomers get anywhere
from $5 to $10 more per bath, because of the convenience
they offer the consumer. It also is a business that does not
require any college, although there are grooming schools.
Many, such as Anderson, learn on-the-job. (Some states,
such as New Jersey, have recently passed legislation requir-
ing any groomer who utilizes "poisons" to pass a test.)

Anderson, a high school dropout who loved animals,
built her business quickly and carved a niche by focusing
on the environment and the relatively healthy-type bath she
offers. She has billed herself as the "all-natural mobile
groomer," and in today's environment where there is a
major concern over toxins, it has given her a marketing
advantage. (Additionally, she does not have to take a test or
pay a fee for utilizing poisons, should her state adopt a law
similar to the one in New Jersey.)

Mobile grooming has been around for a long time, Anderson explains:

> . . . but the pressure on people for their time has
> helped us. People want convenience and they do not
> want their pets to go through a trauma. When they
> take them to a grooming shop, it is difficult for the
> animal to adjust, especially when the owner leaves.
> Most animals do not like baths, and when you com-
> pound that with the strange, away from home envi-
> ronment, it is tough on the pet. Owners understand
> and they see mobile grooming as a viable alterna-
> tive.

Anderson bathes the pets with all-natural products. The
animals will never be harmed through harsh chemicals,
and Anderson's insurance, which she carries in the event an

animal becomes ill and needs attention, is less because she does not use toxic chemicals.

Mobile groomers have another advantage over the store groomer—liability. Groomers in stores or retail outlets have to carry liability insurance in the event a customer slips and falls while in the shop. It happens. When it does, liability rates soar. Usually, the client never enters a mobile groomer's van. They're outside, handing the leash that is fastened to the animal, to the groomer.

One trade association estimates that within the next ten years, more than 10 percent of the animals groomed will be handled via a mobile salon.

Anderson says:

> When I started it was a difficult business, because many people in my area had never seen or even heard of a mobile groomer. Some even thought I just picked up the animal and delivered them to the grooming shop.
>
> I had to knock on doors, but once I got my first two or three animals, I had referrals and repeat customers. Today I don't even solicit new business. It all comes in automatically.

Mobile grooming can be an automatic cash register. Anderson works five to six days a week, gets an average of $40 for grooming (bathing and cutting), and it takes her around 15 minutes to bathe and another 15 to 20 minutes to groom and dry the animal. Because of the convenience, she can charge more.

As the business has grown, she has hired high school kids to help her bathe, while she does the grooming. In many cases, mobile groomers do the bathing and hire a professional to do the cutting and grooming. Anderson took the opposite approach. She did not want to take someone (a groomer) along and only earn about 40 percent of what he or she made. She preferred to train kids, pay them a good part-time wage, and do the grooming (and keep the additional money) herself.

Although the kids take longer, she still nets around $32 per wash. With grooming, she grosses a couple of hundred dollars a day and more than $1,000 a week. That's with one van and one bather, "and I still can't get around to all the people who want my service."

MANUFACTURER'S REP

Thank the changing attitudes, trends, and the way Americans do business for this emerging new service business. It is primarily the rise of the superstores in industries ranging from publishing to hardware that has created the relatively new opportunity of manufacturer's rep.

Superstores have led to the demise of the neighborhood hardware store and small home building centers. They have been replaced by supercenters such as Home Depot and Home Base. The home centers carry three to four times (or more) the merchandise than the smaller building and hardware centers carried.

With that much stock, manufacturers expected to gain the opportunity to place more merchandise. The home centers were also heavy advertisers, which meant they would draw more customers and sell greater amounts of a manufacturer's products.

Problems, however, developed. Home centers do not want to deal with the traditional distributor—they prefer to buy direct from manufacturers. In fact, they will not carry a manufacturer's product line unless they can purchase directly, thus avoiding the middleman, the distributor, and the percentage that costs.

This policy put manufacturers in a difficult position. If they cut off distributors from major accounts, the distributors might refuse to carry product lines to smaller stores. In order to get their goods into the home centers, nearly all manufacturers have capitulated and now sell directly to the centers. Although they are resentful, distributors have come to accept the procedure as a fact of life. Any store that can purchase large quantities of goods can buy direct and cut out the middleman.

Lana McKendry knew the demands and buying power that the centers possessed. Manufacturers needed representatives, or reps.

Reps were not new to industry. Manufacturers in every industry hire them to visit accounts and take orders.

Usually the rep turns in the orders and the manufacturer compensates him or her with a percentage, and then turns the order over to a distributor who fills it.

McKendry saw the rep opportunity, but also realized the business was changing. The home centers not only wanted to cut out the middleman (distributor), but they wanted to eliminate additional costs by having manufacturers take responsibility for stocking and displaying product as well. This was a great opportunity for manufacturers— if they had the personnel to visit the stores.

Today that procedure is a fact of life. If manufacturers want their products bought and displayed in a chain of home centers, they have to be prepared to supply people to handle the stocking and merchandising of the articles.

Manufacturers had a tremendous need—not only for reps, but for an organization that could follow up and handle the stocking and displays, as well. Traditionally, reps never handled product. They just turned in orders.

McKendry created a rep company and offered manufacturers stocking and display services, as well. (Interestingly, the demand for someone just to stock and display has become so great that specialized stocking and display businesses have emerged. Many reps hire these companies to handle the in-store duties, and the reps compensate them from the fees the manufacturer pays. Ultimately, McKendry hired one of these companies to handle her in-store stocking/display needs.) In three years McKendry has built an enterprise that had revenues of more than $20 million last year. A rep will collect anywhere from a low of 2 to a high of 15 percent on sales from a manufacturer.

McKendry says:

> There's an advantage to handling the in-store merchandising. If you are in the store and set up your own displays, you are able to put something together that is eye-catching. Normally, when store personnel do it themself, the person doing the stocking is inexperienced. They don't know how to make a display attractive. We do, and with our approach the manufacturers sell more merchandise, and we get more orders—and commission.

The changes in the home building/home center industry are indicative of what is happening in other retail-oriented businesses. Giant superstores are coming in, and, with their buying power, they are able to eliminate the middleman and put more demands on manufacturers. The opportunity for other entrepreneurs familiar with those industries is there.

But breaking into these industries takes time and, as McKendry says:

> dues. You have to know the players. In this industry, for instance, there is a core of merchandise buyers. You have to get to know them, and once you do you find they do not change much. They may go from one chain to another, but the tendency is for the chain to hire someone who is experienced and knows the industry. It is tough for a new buyer to break in. If they leave one chain, you can rely upon

them popping up at another within a few weeks. The industry is similar to baseball and football. Today, if a professional football coach or baseball manager leaves one team, it is a certainty that within a short time period he will be occupying a similar spot with another team. The home center industry works in the same. In order to be successful, a manufacturer's rep has to get to know the players—that is, the merchandise buyers—at every home center.

Establishing a rep business is not costly. In fact, a typical expenditure can be under $2,000, but it takes time to make the contacts and build a rep business. Reps are not on salary or a draw. They earn commissions.

Says McKendry: "It's tough to get started, because nobody pays you. You have to learn the business by working at a home center . . . see how they buy . . . learn how the purchasing people operate . . . and learn who they are. Once you do, you are ready."

THE NEW CONSULTING OPPORTUNITY

If the 1980s are remembered for anything, it will be the failure of the savings & loan industry and the equally dismal performance of banking as a whole.

No other industry had as much turmoil, failure, merger, and poor publicity as banking. Once considered the pillar of the community, bankers were becoming known as the anchor dragging down the country's financial well-being.

Compounding the image and problems were the number of executives who were accused and convicted of wrongdoing. By the end of the decade, banking was in a shambles, it had been downsized, and virtually every banking institution was shorthanded.

The industry might have survived the drastic cuts were it not for increased government regulation. It wasn't long before the federal government monitored bankers' every turn and move. Suddenly many banking institutions found themselves faced with complex paperwork and requirements, yet they lacked an experienced staff that could handle what was needed.

In the midst of the turmoil, layoffs, and restructuring was opportunity and Dennis McCuistion. McCuistion, who had more than 20 years of banking experience, filled a void. While most in the industry pondered the new regulations, he knew the requirements and how to fulfill them thoroughly. He was the epitome of many consultants who found the tail end of the 1980s and the 1990s to be the perfect time to be in the consulting field. Companies in every industry were shorthanded, and they were willing to pay well for the right assistance.

Like many "failure-proof" entrepreneurs, McCuistion had the experience and the background to build a successful business. He knew the industry and was aware of the problems long before banking executives even saw them. He says:

> Banking is going to have to rely upon outside help for quite a while. In many ways, banks are no different than other industries. Everyone is cutting back and hoping to make do with a thin staff. When they run into trouble, they call a consultant. That's why I believe the 1990s is going to be the golden era for consulting. There is going to be demand from every industry.

Today the swing is to return to the core. If a company started selling furniture, it is returning to furniture sales, just as software retailers are returning to selling software, appliance makers are concentrating on manufacturing appliances, and so on. Diversification is out and core is in.

VALET PARKING

Credit the rising cost of worker's compensation and the need for service for the resurgence of a relatively old enterprise that exists in every city—valet parking. Valet parking is a business that has been around for years, but few take notice of it. For those who do, however, it has become a profitable venture with little risk and high profitability.

With the growing worker's comp problems, many restaurants, malls, theaters, and exhibit halls shy away from offering valet parking themselves because of potential legal problems. Most of these facilities do not want to hire their own parking attendants because of the impact it will have on their insurance rates and the potential for injury.

Vicky Harrington, who started her service more than five years ago with an investment of less than $2,000, finds it is a business with enormous potential if the "valet parking lot owners use modern technology, hire the right labor, and pursue the most profitable accounts."

The most difficult part of the business is hiring dependable workers and convincing clients they can use your service. Hiring is a problem because most of those parking the cars are part-time college students, who may not show up on a Friday or Saturday evening. Harrington found a way around that. She offers her workers better-than-minimum wages. With the higher salary, the workers' dependability increased remarkably.

To generate clients, she offered splits ranging from 20 to 60 percent of the gross fees generated in the lot. For restaurant owners, the extra revenue is like found money.

For the venture to be profitable (this year Harrington

will gross around $60,000 before taxes), a parking lot service owner has to investigate the restaurant or other facility carefully and determine accurately how many patrons the facility can hold, how often customers turn over, how much can be charged, what the split is, and how much the parking attendant earns. That's where technology comes into play. Harrington computerizes everything and calculates—before she bids on a job—how much profit she can make from each establishment.

Profitability is dependent on turnover and how much the valet service owner is paying in splits. In a small, 50-table restaurant, customers could turn over three times an evening, meaning each table would turn three times. In many restaurants that translates to 150 cars—or does it?

"You have to be aware that not everyone is going to use valet services," says Harrington. "In most cases you may only be looking at 100 cars, versus the 150 potential. That can be the difference between a significant profit and a huge loss."

Valet parking fees can run anywhere from $1 to $2 to more than $5. It depends on the market. Typically, in large urban areas, the fees will be higher. Also upping the tariff will be the difficulty of parking elsewhere. For a downtown restaurant, for instance, on-the-street parking may not be an option. In that case, the automobile is a captive of the parking lot. Calculating the potential returns is relatively easy: the number of turnovers per night times the number of tables equals the number of automobiles, minus 10 percent for those who arrive with more than two in an automobile.

In some downtown venues, parking can cost $6 to $10. For instance, many downtown music centers and/or theaters easily generate $6 and $7 per automobile. Harrington says:

The problem with something that is going to

gross big dollars is that you are going to be competing with a large agency that controls numerous parking facilities, or the venue owner may decide to pay the worker's comp and hire his own parking lot attendants. In most cases, it's the former competitor you are faced with.

To build her business, Harrington stayed away from the large conglomerate competitors and concentrated on smaller restaurants, malls, and special events.

She has carefully examined the fee structure, too. If the fee is, for instance, $2 to park, the attendant gets $1 and the other is split between the restaurant and valet parking service owner.

"That means you cannot afford to give the restaurant more than 25 percent, and you are only generating $100 for the attendants. At that rate you could not afford to hire more than two, assuming you give each $50. Even then the venture may not pay off if you do not get the three turns per night."

For Harrington it has paid off. In three years, her earnings have climbed steadily, and she has assembled a stable crew of valet parking attendants. Most important, "I've learned how to judge traffic flow and how many customers will be coming in and out of a restaurant or event. If you can do that, you learn quickly that this can be a profitable business with extremely low start-up costs."

Part of the costs are uniforms ("rent them, it is cheaper to get them cleaned"), an answering and/or voice mail system, and a card system for tracking the automobiles, plus insurance.

If you get drivers with a clean record, your costs will not be significant. The key to the entire business, however, is judging traffic. Being able to determine what your flow is and, of course, convincing owners to retain your service. Once they do, they remain loyal. This is not a high turnover business, insofar as accounts. If you are doing well, owners do not want a strange new parking concessionaire coming in that they know little about.

It is also about carving a niche. At first, a valet service shouldn't target the large venues. Harrington advises: "Stick to the smaller venues and learn there. Make your mistakes with them. After a time, you'll be ready to go after the larger facilities . . . in the next year, that's exactly what I'm planning on doing."

SMALL BUSINESS ADVERTISING/PR

While the shift in the economy has caused most industries to downsize, it also has been the impetus behind a huge resurgence in the number of small businesses that are opening daily. The influx of out-of-work white- and blue-collar workers, college graduates who cannot find a home in a huge corporation, and a growing number of immigrants who see entrepreneurship as the only way to prosper have all combined to create a demand and another "failure-proof" business—advertising and marketing services.

Advertising and promotion is critical to business survival, yet most small business owners fly by the seat of their pants when it comes to marketing and developing consistent plans to bring in customers. In today's competitive business arena, that can be disastrous.

Small businesses are at a special disadvantage regarding marketing. Owners usually have knowledge of their industry and/or trade, but they may not know how to market and promote the enterprise. Most do an occasional flyer, some direct mail stuffed into an envelope, and do not have the expertise to work the "back end"—that is, to generate additional business from their current customers.

Bob Levinson, a high-priced account executive at an advertising agency, found himself out of work when his firm lost a major account. For some time Levinson had been worried about his future with the agency, and he had contingency plans. Instead of jumping back into the Madison Avenue environment, he planned to open his own small agency—one that would cater exclusively to the small business person who could not afford the high-priced agency expertise but needed help.

Most agencies shy away from pursuing small business accounts because they know the dollars are not there. Still, many small businesses grow into large enterprises—and accounts.

Levinson saw the potential. The major difference between his approach and that of major agencies was that he would not ask for a retainer. Small businesses could not afford to pay one. Instead, he structured a "menu-based service" that is rapidly spreading across many industries. With a menu, clients pick what they want, and each item (service) has a price tag. This approach is affordable for businesses that do not have the capital for complete service.

Levinson charged $X for an advertisement, $XX for a brochure, and so on. The owners knew they paid only for what they ordered. If they needed additional consulting services revolving around strategies and marketing tactics, they could buy an hour or two of Levinson's time, as well.

Levinson kicked off his business by visiting a local mall and making appointments with the owners of all the independently owned outlets. He also stopped at two large commercial centers in the area that held manufacturers and distribution outlets.

In two weeks Levinson had signed up ten merchants and three manufacturers. At the initial appointment he also discussed budget, so he had an idea of what each business had to spend.

By the end of his first month, he had generated $800 in revenue. After the third month, his monthly income was averaging $2,000, and in six months he was working for enough clients to bring in nearly $4,000. By that time he had also hired a part-time assistant and secretary.

"Small business people," he says, "can be like any major client. They need the help and are willing to pay for it. You have to determine budgets, of course, so you do not go overboard. In more than a year of working with them, I have not had a problem, and several are beginning to grow into large clients."

Levinson says most advertising/promotion specialists opening their own business go after the "large client—the major retailer or company that can afford to pay the overhead. Chances are you will not get this account, because they are big enough to go to a large agency. Seldom will they fool with a one-man shop. Small businesses, however, will."

By small, Levinson gives some examples.

One business may only need a news release or a brochure. I've set it up so that I charge them a fee per release and a flat fee for the brochure. You cannot grow significantly on the basis of one or even a dozen clients. The key behind the small business advertising/promotion service is to work for 30 or 40 clients. They all won't be giving you work at the same time, but with that many there is a constant flow of jobs to be done. When they do grow into larger accounts, if you have provided premium service, they will stick with you. You won't lose them to the larger agencies. Start small, keep your overhead low, and do a lot of networking. Ask your clients for referrals. Those who are pleased know 10 or 20 other businesspeople, businesspeople who almost always turn into another client.

MAID SERVICES

Of all personal service businesses, maid service has one of the best potentials to build as an enterprise because of the mistakes that most fledgling companies in the industry make. Typically, maid service firms send one or two workers (if it is two, the consumer gets a three- or four-hour shift instead of a six- or eight-hour shift), and they start cleaning. Some services refuse to do windows, while others have different restrictions.

Maid service firms do not keep clients long because their main interest appears to be how fast maids can clean and how much they can make. For a four-hour shift, a fee of $40 to $60 is not unusual. The owner of the maid service business pays the workers anywhere from $20 to $40 for their efforts.

Delia Ornaz worked for a maid service company for two years before she decided to strike out on her own. Her area was Orange County, California, a relatively affluent section of southern California that had an abundance of households with two breadwinners. Ornaz's first job was generated from a sign she had posted in a neighborhood supermarket. That client referred her to a friend, and the process continued until she had six clients a week and a gross income of $300 for four and one-half hours of work per day. Her start-up cost was under $100.

That was the start of Ornaz's business venture, but it was far from the finish. She learned several things about customers. First, most maid service companies did not consult the clients before they sent the cleaners into the home. They assumed. Ornaz never did.

She walked through the property with each client and found out the areas considered most urgent and important. Ornaz marked them on a priority list, and used her past experience to dictate exactly how much time it would take a clean the various parts of the house.

When they were finished with the walkthrough, Ornaz quoted a price for the cleaning and told the client how long she thought it would take. After cleaning, Ornaz consulted with the client and asked her to walk through the home to see if it was done properly. The woman was amazed at the request.

Ornaz recalls:

> This particular client had about a half-dozen different maid services, and none ever asked her what she thought of the finished product. I just did it accidentally, but I learned it was real important when it came to satisfying customers. Usually where you get the complaints is when you clean and leave, and people do not get a chance to inspect. For the most part, they do not want to criticize your work, but they would like to look and see if the important things were done.

Ornaz used the same techniques in every home, and within a few months she had more properties to clean than she could handle. "I could see the potential," she recalls, "to make more money if I could get someone to help." She did. Ornaz found another woman and trained her to do as good a job as she did.

"People laugh when I tell them I trained someone to clean house, but it is necessary," Ornaz emphasizes. "Not everyone cleans the same, nor are they as thorough. I wanted to make sure that anyone I put in a home would do a good job. I wanted the repeat business and the referrals."

Ornaz works on a commission basis, and the people she trains and places in cleaning situations give her 20 percent of their gross.

Most maid services take 50 percent or more from

the person doing the cleaning. That's foolish. All you do is make them anxious to go out on their own. By taking a smaller percentage, I have a group of happier workers. They don't have to worry about generating business—I do that. And they get to clean the same homes each week. Once you get used to it, things get easier.

Ornaz has her workers pay for supplies. If they need transportation, she supplies it. To date, she has eight people working five days a week. Each generates approximately $300 to $350, with Delia taking 20 percent of the gross as her fee for lining up the client.

Ornaz says:

I don't think I'll become a millionaire but I've found a business that can earn me some good income, and I'm my own boss. One of the things you have to remember, though, is to talk to the homeowners. I communicate with the clients. I find out what the owners expect, so they are never disappointed. And find out what your workers want, and let them know what you expect. If you do that, this business is great.

PARKING LOT STRIPING

Now let's consider another business for which there is a constant demand, that is immune to the ups and downs of the economy, that is necessary, that has no advertising cost, and that has potential clients, both private and public sector, in every city and town in the country.

During his seven years in business, Jerry Turner has provided striping for businesses ranging from the neighborhood minimall to large shopping complexes. He's even gotten state contracts. And today two-thirds of his customers are repeat business.

Turner says that although the field is labor intensive, the opportunities are endless.

"Just look around and you will see a parking lot somewhere that has striping. One striper with one machine should be able to do $250,000 a year, and his profit would be somewhere around $75,000. Expand the business and get help, and you'll do better."

References are the key. "Do a job right, and the owner will refer you. Blow it, and you don't get anything." One way to blow it is to use inferior merchandise in an attempt to make more profit. Take paint, for instance.

"Some of it will not stick well if the weather drops under 60 degrees. You've got to be aware of that and buy the right product."

Another way to blow it is to have your equipment break down and not be able to finish a job. That can happen. "It has happened to me," Turner says. "I recommend that anyone getting in the business have a backup unit. Be ready because your customers are not interested in seeing a job half done."

Stripers have another outlet for marketing their services aside from visiting the local mall, shopping center, or doctor's office. "Get to know some of the paving people—that is, the people who repave lots. Once a lot is repaved, it needs striping, and generally repavers don't fool with striping. It's another business and requires different machinery. Work a deal with them. Give them a commission or percentage if they bring you in to do the striping."

Follow-up is critical. "You've got to be able to judge when the lot will come due again. Talk to the purchasing agent or whoever is involved. Find out approximately when the job will be bid again, and make sure you're there. In most cases, if the agent or owner is satisfied, there will not be a bid. You'll get the job, just as we do."

Striping is not a job for a novice, says Turner. "You have to learn it, and the best way is to work for someone who is in the striping or paving business. There's a low cash investment, but there is a great deal of time involved before someone learns all the ins and outs."

5

Researching and
Determining the
Market

It happened in the 1970s to one of the auto industry's Big Three. After several years of research and development, the company had developed a deluxe new model that both management and the sales force were convinced would capture a huge share of the luxury car market.

They were even more assured of success because the price tag they were able to put on the model was several thousand dollars below equivalent competitive models.

The new model had been so rushed that the company had bypassed doing the usual pricing research. Even when the sales vice president suggested surveying consumers to determine if the pricing was correct, management objected. They did not want to delay this hot new model. Finally, and reluctantly, however, they agreed to a simple market research price test.

The company held up shipments while a special survey was constructed. All it consisted of was the manufacturer hiring a photographer to take a side and front view of the new car model. From its computerized customer list, the company then pulled a cross-section of 500 previous buyers from throughout the country and hired a market research firm to visit those buyers with the photos of the car and conduct a survey.

Because of deadline pressures, management wanted only two questions answered. Did consumers like the car? And how much would they be willing to pay for it?

When the results were tallied, answers to the first question did not surprise anyone—more than 90 percent loved the design. However, answers to the second amazed everyone from senior management on down—when asked how much they would be willing to pay for the car, the average answer was more than $3,000 *above* what the sticker price would have been. Detroit usually worries about prices that were too high. Seldom are cars priced too low—and management knows that if a product and/or service is priced too low, it can fail.

With this information in hand, the market research firm met with the company's executives and made several critical arguments. First, the car was underpriced. If it was sold at the planned suggested list price, prospective customers might not make the purchase. The reason: Something was probably wrong with the car. Why else would the manufacturer sell it so cheaply? Price helps set a perceived value in customers' minds. Price an item too low, and customers can end up believing something is wrong with it.

Pricing is especially difficult when it comes to service-related businesses. Charge too little and the value of the services—to the customers—may be suspect. In addition, a low price makes the provider's work that much harder to earn a living. (Pricing will be covered in depth in Chapter 6.)

As a result of the market analysis, the manufacturer hiked the price a full $3,000. To this day company executives will tell you that if they had not done so, the model might have been a flop instead of a huge success. They gave consumers what they wanted: a higher price for a (perceived) better automobile.

Consumers—and all customers—have an idea as to what products and services are worth. Goods have a perceived value. Pricing some too high, of course, hurts sales, but pricing goods and services too low also has an impact.

As mentioned, the market research involved in determining price need not be complex. Take Don Kracke's (the inventor of the highly successful consumer product, Ricky-Ticky-Sticky). Kracke did his research by first packaging the product, knocking on doors in his area, showing people the product, explaining what it was, and asking them one question: How much would you be willing to pay for this package? He simply took the average answer and priced his product accordingly.

The predecessor to *Entrepreneur* magazine was *Insider's Report*, a monthly magazine that went only to members of Insider's Report Association. The magazine carried a $7.50 price tag and was billed as the "world's most expensive magazine"—and it was. Members of the association did not pay $7.50 a copy, because it came as part of their membership. Still, the perceived value—in their eyes—was $7.50, and it was worth the price because of the in-depth, exclusive reports only association members could get.

When the publication was renamed *Entrepreneur* and it was sold on newsstands, the price tag was lowered to $2.95. The most difficult part of the transition was convincing former subscribers they had not been ripped off with the prior, higher price—a price they never actually paid, but one that had perceived value attached to it.

The company surveyed members prior to the price reduction and found out how they felt. They knew there would be problems. To alleviate any hard feelings, the company extended its customer's memberships (and magazine issues) at no cost.

CONDUCTING UNCOMPLICATED RESEARCH

Thus, research need not be complicated or sophisticated. The automobile manufacturer surveyed previous customers. Doing so made sense. If they bought before, chances are they are prime prospects to buy again. If you want to find out what people will buy and how much they will pay, there is no better source than previous customers. If the company and its products and/or services are new, ask those who bought similar merchandise or services from competitors.

A few years ago Chuck Laufer, a well-known publisher of teenage magazines, watched as his revenues soared as young girls purchased his publications in order to get a centerfold picture of the latest teen idol, a young, up-and-coming singer—Donny Osmond.

Laufer studied the picture of Donny and looked at other pictures of teen idols. Suddenly it occurred to him that the idols all looked alike. Each was dark-haired and thin, and had a number of other similar characteristics. He knew that every time one of these idols came on the scene, his sales soared. If he could find a young man who looked like the Donny Osmonds of the world, he might be able to create his own idol.

To find the idol, he ran a "look-a-like" contest in his magazines. He invited readers to submit photographs of young men who "resembled Donny Osmond." Pictures came in by the hundreds. To test the appeal of those who looked promising, Laufer ran the photos in his magazines. Traditionally, if readers liked what they saw, they wrote letters. If they did not, they failed to respond.

One young man received hundreds of letters, enough to convince the publisher that he "had the makings of another teen idol." He flew the youngster to Hollywood, shot additional pictures, did more testing in the magazines, and received an even greater response.

Within 12 months, Laufer had the young man record a song, and a label released the recording. The record, "Heartbeat, It's a Lovebeat," became a hit and sold 2.5 million copies. The young man became a star and teen idol, and during the next 18 months millions of dollars' worth of products were sold by Tony DeFranco, a 13-year-old from Canada who was test-marketed by his photo appearing in a magazine.

A decade later Laufer found another potential teen idol named Michael Damian. He repeated the same test, and this time he created a teenager who went on to become first an idol, then a star in CBS-TV's *Young & Restless* and later on Broadway in *Joseph's Technicolor Dream Coat*.

Testing of both these young stars was not sophisticated. Magazine consumers were asked only one question (via a photo): Do you like what you see? Their answer gave Chuck Laufer and his company two products that went on to sell millions.

That's the way all teen idols, from Frank Sinatra to David Cassidy, were created. Consumers (teenage girls) were shown pictures through newspapers and magazines, and made their decision. No sophisticated, psychological tests were constructed, and with most products none are needed.

SUCCESSFUL RESEARCH TECHNIQUES

Asking previous or present (or prospective) customers is the best way to test a product. One thing to keep in mind— everything changes.

Creating a product and/or service that has universal need does not mean that it will sell. Michael Grant, an insurance broker, devised a much-needed board with adjustable straps that could be used by young (or old) patients when they were receiving intravenous medication.

There was nothing like it around. Grant was sure he was onto a super invention that would sell. He spent about $15,000 trying to convince people that it would and has been issued two patents, with a third pending. Still, he was unable to market the product until the Oklahoma Commerce Department's Inventors' Assistance Program helped him find a small medical products company to license the armboard. Grant's royalty is 7.5 percent but, as yet, there have not been any sales.

Next to manufacturing, inventions are the hardest products to get off the ground. If research has been done and there is a need, the most feasible way of marketing a new innovative product is to license it. For a newcomer, to manufacture and distribute a new product, it can cost millions, while licensing represents only a fraction of the cost. All it takes is a prototype and research.

Many established manufacturers simply place market research people in a supermarket to determine likes and dislikes of their proposed new products. After a dozen or so people are asked their opinion, trends, and preferences can be discerned.

An automobile manufacturer, Ricky-Ticky-Stickies, a business and a teenage magazine may seem to be worlds apart, but they are not, especially when it comes to research and determining if a product is viable. Aside from need and pricing, there are critical questions that every "failure-proof" business owner in this book answered before they launched their product or service.

- Does the product/service exist?
- If it does, where?
- How long has it been out there?
- Is it successful?

Products/services that are already on the market are proven. If people want to introduce the same—or a similar—product or service, they have a greater chance of success than if the product is revolutionary and new. If it is already on the market, it has already been tested.

SOME PRODUCTS REJECTED BECAUSE OF ATTITUDES

Every industry has examples of the new products that may just be too revolutionary for buyers. The electronic price scanners found in every supermarket were originally introduced in the Midwest more than 30 years ago. Checkers refused to use them because they did not understand how some "electronic gadget" could possibly be as accurate as they were when it came to punching in prices. They refused to accept going from a manual register to an electronic scanner. The change was too revolutionary.

Part of the reason for that attitude is the culture differences we have in different areas of the country. The electronic cash register was first introduced in Chicago, and the Midwest is traditionally conservative, slow to change. It does not accept new ideas easily.

Tune-up shops emerged in the 1970s, as an outgrowth of the early 1970 gas shortages. Gas stations were firing mechanics, and with the higher price of gasoline, their interest turned primarily to pumping gas. Soon they even abandoned "full service" and gave consumers the option of paying a higher price for it. Today, of course, few stations even offer the higher priced full service.

Tune-up shops debuted on the West Coast, in California. It took several years before the concept spread to the Midwest and eventually across the country. It was another illustration of the West—and parts of the Southeast (Florida), New York, and Hawaii—being more open to new and unique concepts. Much of the acceptance has to do with the population. All those areas are melting pots of immigrants and cultures. They accept change more readily. Areas in which the population is more homogeneous, such as the Midwest, are less receptive to new products and ideas.

In the late 1970s, computer stores developed. Once again, they were welcomed with open arms in California. It took several years before these new retail outlets spread to the Midwest and portions of the South. Wherever there is a mixture of people, new ideas are more acceptable.

On the West Coast, a young housewife worked with a laboratory to develop a shampoo that would kill fleas on animals without poison. The idea was difficult to accept, and when the product was developed, tested, and proven, many refused to believe it would work.

The housewife thought she had a tool that every groomer—and consumer—would welcome. Her shampoo was also an environmental plus, since it did not contain any of the harmful poisons that would pollute the water supply.

Introducing the product was not easy. After years of being accustomed to poisons, people were slow to accept the idea that something else could kill fleas. Even when the product went through Environmental Protection Agency (EPA) testing and proved it killed as well as any poison, there was still resistance.

Purchasing agents from stores who had customers request "nonpoisonous" killers had a difficult time believing the new product could measure up to the poisons. Even veterinarians, who were educated and realized that chemically it would be possible to utilize something other than poisons, were skeptical. The greatest acceptance came about on the West Coast, with its heterogeneous population, its acceptance of new products, and its overriding interest in the environment.

REVOLUTIONARY IDEAS ARE HARD SELLS

The entrepreneur with the revolutionary idea has two strikes against them. It's easier to stay with the tried and proven, much as the synthetic jewelry manufacturer did. His product was the same as hundreds of other manufacturers before him, but he developed a new way to market the stones. Marketing made the difference, not improvements in the product.

Anything new, revised, or remodeled always should be tested. New services should be researched, too. In

Blingbrook, Illinois, and Indianapolis, Indiana, two gas stations currently are testing "self-cleaning" bathrooms. Engineer Glenwood Garvey invented the self-cleaner after hearing horror stories about the conditions of gas station rest rooms. Garvey designed the unit by imagining the bathroom was a giant dishwasher. Against one wall is the sink and toilet, with a vertical hinge in the center of the sink/toilet to enable the corners to pivot in. Inside, more than three dozen nozzles spray cleanser and water at walls, mirrors, sinks, and toilet. Warm air dries the room when the cleaning is completed, and the time required for a complete wash and dry is 24 minutes.

Consumer market testing has been done, and in nearly every case the person quizzed has said they would purchase one for their own home. Of course, it will be three to five years before the consumer version is ready; however, the concept has gained acceptance because it is not revolutionary. It is simply an improvement on an existing product—the typical bathroom.

DETERMINING THE REAL NEEDS

Equally as important as familiarity is need. Do people need the product/service? The overly enthusiastic inventor of the clay brick cited in an earlier chapter is an example of need and acceptance. In his case, there was not a need, nor was there credibility.

In southern California an entrepreneur looked at a huge, empty building on the west side of Los Angeles and came up with a money-making idea. He turned it into a "Chic & Cheap Emporium," a retail center devoted to antique and hand-crafted shops. By themselves, none of the retailers could afford to rent a structure like the Emporium, but together they can afford it. The landlord rents the 7,000-

square-foot Emporium to 48 different entrepreneurs. They pay $10 to $20 a square foot, at a cost of $100 or more per space. The owner also collects 10 percent commission on all sales.

Sound familiar? The concept is not new, but this landlord put a twist to it. Inside, aside from merchandise, there is a cappuccino bar, and with its proximity to Beverly Hills it has turned into a celebrity hangout. It's the place to go—and buy. The "in" spot.

At the same time, the landlord has filled a need for the 48 entrepreneurs. He's providing a reasonably priced retail outlet with good traffic. By themselves, none of the entrepreneurs could have rented/leased the entire building, but by splitting it up, the landlord solved the problem and, of course, filled a need. Need is the key.

A man may want a new automobile, but his five-year-old model has been problem-free. He does not really need one. A housewife may want a maid, but she may not need one or be able to afford the service.

The entrepreneurs already discussed all have one thing in common: Their services filled a void—a need. Lana McKendry, for example, who became a highly successful manufacturer's rep, did just that. Manufacturers desperately needed her services, and she knew it from the experience she had in the industry. She had firsthand knowledge because she worked for a home center and on many occasions she heard manufacturers bemoaning their fate. Before she actually opened her doors, she talked to several of the manufacturers and asked a simple question: Would they be interested in her rep services, which would also handle in-store merchandising and displays? The overwhelming response convinced her she was onto a good business.

Dennis McCuistion also filled a void. Bankers who had lost valuable employees because of downsizing no longer had employees with the expertise to fulfill the federal government's reporting requirements. McCuistion had already opened his consulting practice when the first banker approached him. It did not take guesswork. The industry was shorthanded and needed someone knowledgeable to assist them with regulations.

Mike Goldberg spotted a publisher's need that was brought on by a tightening economy and the inability of publishers to maintain a staff of in-house sales reps. The larger publications and publishing conglomerates were able to hire, but not the thousands of smaller, barely surviving publications that serviced industries ranging from pets to purchasing. Goldberg tested his premise. He asked publishers within the pet industry if they would retain him. The answer gave him his direction.

They could not afford to hire full-time, in-house advertising salespeople, so they contracted out. They were willing to give him a national exclusive if he could sell ads. Goldberg also saw the need within a specific industry and realized he could service more than one publisher in that industry.

Jay Horoki's janitorial service answered a need for thorough, reasonable, efficient cleaning services. Clients needed someone who was accountable and would clean what they needed, and not what the janitorial service chose. Horoki's experience in the industry was all he needed. He could see the gap and opportunity.

Jerry Turner saw a need for high-quality products and rapid service when he started striping parking lots. Because he had already worked in the industry, he knew the value of dependability and keeping deadlines.

Kendall Shurcut saw the need for owners to leave their animals at a grooming parlor that was nearby and convenient.

Bob Levinson saw the disadvantages small businesses

faced when it came to marketing. They could not afford large ad agency expertise, and no one catered to the small business person. That was the opportunity. More than one small business person told Levinson he wanted to buy just a brochure or just one ad or a news release.

Delia Ornaz worked with clients and saw the lack of service that was provided in the maid service area. It was an opportunity, and she jumped on it.

Chase Revel built *Entrepreneur* into a $15 million empire with a test that cost $44. He was selling advice, and he wanted to know if people would buy it before he took the time to create the publication. His question was answered by the response he received from this small space ad in the *Wall Street Journal*.

> How much money does Joe make? How much money does Joe make in his business? Want to know? Send $X to . . .

Readers responded by the hundreds and Revel sat down and put together the first issue of *Insider's Report*, the 16-page newsletter that was the forerunner of *Entrepreneur*.

Most techniques utilized by these entrepreneurs would not qualify as highly scientific, but they were on target. How can you go wrong asking your customers what they think?

People may not buy a product or service, but they are quick to give opinions. Astute entrepreneurs ask to determine if there really is a demand for their product and/or service.

Each one of these businesspeople positioned their product or service so that it answered a specific need. "Failure-proof" business owners do not sell products or services, they answer needs, and they position their company with that in mind. Kendall Shurcut let his customers know how easy it was to reach his grooming shop and how much he cared for animals. Most of his competitors stressed clean coats, while Shurcut stressed the best care and shampoo available.

Lana McKendry markets her ability to place more of a manufacturer's products in-store because of her relationship with buyers. Dennis McCuistion answers the banker's needs to have a consultant on board to solve some financial problems, and Jerry Turner's reputation for prompt high-quality service and craftsmanship answers his clients' needs to keep customers' inconvenience to a minimum.

Answering needs is the basic premise behind all successful enterprises. Insurance salespeople do not market life insurance policies. Instead, they provide "protection" for the policyowner and his or her family. That's what the buyer needs. Clothing stores do not sell overcoats, they sell warmth and comfort.

INFLUENCE OF CHANGING LIFESTYLES

Needs change frequently, and those changes give entrepreneurs a clue as to what products and services the market will buy. Driving these changes and the success of new products and services is a radical switch in lifestyle and attitudes of consumers. Each of these changes provides a clue as to why some businesses become "failure-proof" while others miss the mark.

In the 1980s, consumers consumed and their debt rose rapidly. The so-called baby boomers were in their prime earning years and helped drive the economy with the purchase of heavy durable goods—everything from BMWs to vacations in exotic, faraway places. Toward the end of the decade, new attitudes started to emerge.

Many people realized that if they wanted families, they

had to do it before they got too old. They married, settled down, and became concerned with paying off debt instead of incurring more.

In 1990, the U.S. debt per individual had reached one of its all-time highs. This decade, however is rapidly becoming one in which debt is being paid off. Consumers are saving, sales of luxury automobiles are down, and money is flowing to the stock market and other areas where investments can be liquid.

Now Jeeps are replacing BMWs. Baby stores are thriving along with toys. Everything is becoming kid and home-oriented. Home gardening has returned, and from two to three gardening catalogs there are now more than two dozen. People are staying home, watching TV, renting videos, and saving money.

Consumers/workers have been impacted by downsizing. They know the corporation may not be there for life, but their family will be. For the first time in many decades, workers are putting family ahead of company. And companies are bending in an effort to get employees to balance both.

Owners and managers of "failure-proof" small businesses are cognizant of these changes, and many have a unique operating philosophy that provides employee flexibility. "As long as the job is done well," says Jay Horoki, "my people can go home early or juggle their schedules. They know I'm interested in having the best janitorial service possible, and if giving them added liberties enables me to do that, I'll do it."

At Microsoft, the country's top personal computer software maker, there are seven-day work weeks—but flexible hours. Bonuses and stock options reward those who put in the time. But Microsoft has a workforce slightly different from that of the typical manufacturer. The average age of workers is 30, only half are married, and only half of those employees have children. Young, single employees are willing to put in extra time building their careers. When they get older, have kids and a family, other considerations become important. Home means more and, today, many workers spend a good deal of time there rather than taking off for weekends.

This trend to an emphasis on home life is a clue for those marketing products and services. The recent merger of QVC and the Home Shopping Network offers a peek at what's coming and what some of the major manufacturers and marketers of products and services foresee.

Home Shopping, which generates revenue from selling merchandise via television to the consumer is going upscale and high tech. It is selling expensive gold jewelry as well as high fashion, and telephone purchases will top $2 billion this year. Retailers such as Saks Fifth Avenue and designers such as Diane von Furstenberg are going on QVC (another home shopping-type network) to sell their wares.

The success of these networks is not merely a matter of offering time-saving, convenient shopping. Research went into how to sell on-screen, and QVC and the Home Shopping Network follow certain rules. For example, merchandise is always built up so that it appears as if it is "special" and available for only a limited time. Many of the bargain prices are possible because these networks buy direct from manufacturers and they are not subject to purchasing through distributors.

Apparel is usually in primary colors, because complicated patterns appear fuzzy on TV. Large sizes sell well, and in most cases the merchandise is modeled.

Home Shopping, QVC and many other networks utilize celebrities to sell wares, as they are credible and their presence glamorizes the product. The major drawback—the customers cannot touch and feel the product. But, with money-back guarantees, hosts who demonstrate and become friendly with viewers, and products that are priced properly, the drawbacks are not significant.

Home shopping via TV also utilizes another future trend—fewer employees. Although it takes people to man the telephones and ship the merchandise, the growth of technology will ultimately lead to fewer employees at the retail level. The clerk of today may be gone tomorrow. Much of this downsizing is being driven not only by technology but by necessity, as well. Soaring health insurance and other employee costs are causing most companies to take good, hard long looks at their staffing.

Barry Diller, who built Fox Broadcasting, is guiding both QVC and Home Shopping and is convinced the enterprise will be a trillion-dollar-plus business within a few years. The retail business is entering a new phase, and television is going to become an increasingly active competitor. The question that is on most retailer's minds: Will these electronic shopping outlets be the future of the retail trade?

Aside from QVC and the Home Shopping Network, which reach more than 100 million shoppers, in 1993 alone "infomercials" sold close to $1 billion worth of merchandise. Some retailers even have their own cable-TV channels. Nordstrom's, an upscale department store, is working on an interactive TV screen that will allow consumers to have conversations with a "personal shopper" who will cater to their needs.

At the same time, the population continues to grow and the roads become more clogged. All this leads to one conclusion—retailing is going to experience drastic changes, and anyone contemplating a retail outlet should examine trends carefully before taking the plunge.

In a few years shoppers will be able to purchase most of their goods via some type of interactive television. Consumers will be able to punch a button and order direct. Even grocery shopping lends itself to interactive shopping and delivery.

Chase Revel, who was the first to forecast accurately that computer stores and tune-up shops would be household words long before they were established, says "technology and changing attitudes will continue to drive these trends and new businesses. Entrepreneurs should look closely at them and see if their businesses 'fit.' " That is, will they fit in the future; will they be viable?

Revel uses the example of enterprises such as travel agencies. Many consumers use ATMs (automatic teller machines), but now there is another electronic wizard on line—ETMs (electronic ticket machines). These machines, which can ticket someone for any event, are beginning to get mass distribution. And before long they will be in hotel lobbies, banks, and hundreds of other convenient locations, locations that will market travel as well as other type tickets. What impact will ETMs have on travel agents? Could they make travel agencies obsolete?

As this book is being written, another major trend is taking shape in the real estate industry. Agents are being equipped with laptop computers that actually have film and soundtracks on them. The agent simply takes the laptop to a consumer, who can narrow their choice for a home without ever leaving their living rooms thanks to these computerized descriptive tours.

Many of these trends are being driven by the consumers' desire to save time and shop more conveniently. For the past few years, the average time shoppers spend in malls has dropped but, at the same time, the average dollar purchase they made during that stay has increased. Clearly consumers have less time and are not merely browsing through the mall. Only teenagers treat the mall differently: They view malls as social gathering spots. But teenagers do not buy a significant amount of goods.

POSITIONING

Successful products and services have USPs—that is, unique selling propositions. There is something different about them that is conveyed to customers, and most of the time that difference is more perceived than real. Astute businesspeople find a USP and market it to their customers. Consumer products and services that best fulfill needs fall into two general categories—they appeal to the consumer's (or buyer's) ego or promise him/her some financial gratification (greed).

Automobile dealers who can somehow convince prospects that a vehicle will enhance their image stand a better chance of selling one. In typical automobile ads, on network television, the advertisers concentrate on appealing to the prospect's ego. That is, in the film the buyer of the car gets the girl too.

Marketers of financial products do not usually appeal to "saving for a rainy day" or retirement but to the prospect's sense of greed by saying: "We can make you financially independent." That means rich. Everyone wants a relatively safe investment, but people respond to greed quicker and with greater intensity than to safety.

The product/service also has to be affordable. In the 1990s consumers (and customers) are more cost-conscious than ever. The frugality is being dictated in part by the aging baby boomers and in part by a growing segment of the population that fails to discern any appreciable difference in Brand X versus Brand Y. Certainly, Coca-Cola, Pepsi-Cola, and other brands associated with a certain taste or quality are retaining market share. But when generic products can be substituted easily, consumers are reaching for them.

Procter & Gamble, one of the giant consumer product manufacturers in the country, has watched some of its leading brands slowly decline. Gaining in popularity are generic products that promise the same benefits. Everything from cigarettes to toothpaste has suffered as consumers reach for cheaper generics. During the past few years P&G and other big companies have flooded the market with coupons and retailers with discounts, only to find that they still continue to lose market share. What these companies have discovered is that if they eliminate the needless incentives and promotions to retailers—in other words, if they cut costs—in many cases their products can compete successfully with generics.

The P&G case is an excellent lesson in economics for entrepreneurs. In the past, many name-brand products were able to hold on to their customers when they hiked prices; today customers are more likely to switch. Why? Customers have become extremely price sensitive, especially when there does not appear to be any major difference in products.

There are exceptions. Take, for instance, Hewlett-Packard. For years the electronic company has made its mark with laser printers, but it had been unable to seize any significant share of the computer market. Then, suddenly, HP came out with a subnotebook-size, portable computer that runs up to ten hours on four AA batteries.

Weighing in under three pounds, the computer, called an OmniBook, has caused a sensation in the industry despite the fact it carries a price tag of around $2,000. Orders indicate that it will be one of the top-ten sellers in the industry.

COMPETITIVE PRICING

What does this teach us? When your products and services are not noticeably different from others—such as P&G's—you must be price competitive. But when your product has significantly different features and improved benefits from those of its competitors, there is much more price elasticity—that is, consumers will pay a higher tab even though the product does basically the same thing as the competitors'.

This fact holds true for small businesses as well as conglomerates. Take Kendall Shurcut, for instance. One of the first things he did when he entered the business was differentiate his product and services.

Shurcut knew that cheaper shampoos did not necessarily ensure the most profit. Many contained less desirable ingredients, were harder to rinse out, and left the animal's coat dull and in poor shape. Therefore, he bought the best, figuring it would be a selling point to his clients.

He also took advantage of the "all-natural" trend, advertising his bathing parlor as an "all-natural" salon where toxic chemicals were never used.

In months Shurcut and his assistants were grooming from twenty to forty dogs a day, at a fee of anywhere from $40 to $60 per animal. Many dogs were regulars—their owners brought them in weekly. Shurcut could charge more even though he was doing basically the same thing every other groomer in town was doing, with one exception. He treated animals special, with all-natural shampoos, and thus protected their health. This perceived difference enabled him to charge more, much as Hewlett-Packard did with its special computer.

Procter & Gamble, Hewlett-Packard, and Kendall Shurcut may seem miles apart, but the research they put into the pricing of their products was similar. All three surveyed the market, determined what their customers wanted, tailor-made products to fit those needs, and charged a premium price.

Still, despite the demand, there *is* a limit as to what people will pay for products and services. "Failure-proof" business owners carefully evaluate and research those limits, and make sure they are within them.

Shurcut's grooming service may be expensive for people who live in a less affluent area, but for the affluent area in which it is located, it is affordable. Hewlett-Packard's new computer may be expensive compared to competition, but it offers benefits that rivals cannot match. Both Shurcut and HP set themselves apart from the crowd.

Mike Goldberg had a brilliant idea—sell space for a variety of magazines all in the same industry—but his customers, the magazine publishers, had to be able to afford his 15 to 20 percent commission. If not, he wouldn't have earned a living.

Before Lana McKendry established her rep business and took on clients, she made sure they could afford to pay her the percentage necessary to keep her doors open and make a profit. Becoming a rep for manufacturers that want to deal with superstores is the beginning of a trend that is going to impact every industry. Smaller retailers are watching the discounts that the superstores are able to obtain when they buy goods, and they are banding together to buy as co-ops. Co-ops need agents and reps, too.

Smaller firms are also trying to upgrade their employees' skills, but they do not have internal training departments. The external trainer who can assist firms in improving productivity and in applying new technology is going to be in demand, as well.

GENERATING REPEAT SALES

Whatever the product and/or service, it has to be affordable. Equally as important, the product or service must be sold to someone over and over again. The enterprise should offer a possibility of repeat business. If it does not, the entrepreneur constantly has to look for new, fresh prospects, which is an exceedingly difficult task. Repeat business enhances the chances for success. An established, "failure-proof" business can generate 50 percent or more of its sales through repeat business. That's one of the keys to the success of these enterprises. People come back.

Can the product and/or service be sold at a profit? Making fresh water from salt is a great idea, but not feasible. Better mousetraps are created daily, but they are not feasible because of cost. Not only do they have to be affordable; they must be priced so the marketer can make a profit. Service people—consultants, groomers, house cleaners, and the like—are selling only one thing: their time. Time is more difficult to price than products, and entrepreneurs have to be careful in arriving at fees. It is easy to charge too much and even easier not to charge enough.

Chase Revel, who has marketed products ranging from synthetic gems to *Entrepreneur* magazine, maintains that entrepreneurs should keep several things in mind when evaluating an enterprise.

> The product or service has to enhance the prospect's life in some way. You also have to determine if people will buy at the price you want. If you are about to offer a service, find out what the competition is charging before you quote prices. See if they are generating customers. Is the demand there? If it is, and the price is right, then you probably will be able to make it.

In the next chapter, we'll take a closer look at pricing.

6

Raising Capital, Pricing, and Billing

Kendall Shurcut, the dog groomer, tells the story calmly, but it is obvious that his experience when he attempted to get financing for his small business taught him something. Shurcut thought he had prepared a complete business plan, covering every aspect of his proposed grooming business.

In it he had carefully detailed his start-up costs, marketing plan, prospective customers, and a five-year forecast. Yet after looking at the plan for a few minutes, the bank loan officer handed it back and asked, "What are you going to use for collateral?"

Shurcut was bewildered. "I'm here for a business loan. I thought I would be able to get one with a business plan that showed how viable this grooming shop could be," he said.

The banker shook his head. "Sorry. We need collateral." The request is commonplace in today's business environment. Regardless of how detailed, thorough, and promising a business plan may be, bankers are hesitant to provide funds to start-up enterprises. Small business is not what it used to be when it comes to financing—and banks are not as loose with capital.

Shurcut found that out, as did most businesspeople who have built "failure-proof" enterprises during the past decade. Banks have plenty of funds for lending, but when it comes to small business, would-be entrepreneurs need more than solid business plans and good credit.

Before the bank failures of the 1980s, capital was readily available to small business people and prospective entrepreneurs. And while in fact more money is available today than at any time in recent history—mostly from consumer savings in liquid investments—it is hard to obtain.

That's why start-up small businesses stand little chance of getting a bank loan any without collateral to back it up. Banks would rather take depositors' funds and place them in mutual fund investments, which in turn are placed in higher yielding stocks, which frequently carry a lower risk. This strategy has enabled most banks to earn handsome profits over the past few years. Why should they open the purse strings?

NEW SOURCE OF REVENUE

That does not mean small business people have no source of outside funds. The Small Business Administration (SBA) received a fresh new influx of funds, but the demand for money is enormous. The agency, which actually guarantees small business loans made by banks, provided a record $5.6 billion during the 1992 fiscal year, an increase of 35 percent over 1991. Applicants have deluged the agency with more than $30 million in requests per day.

Obviously, the SBA doesn't have the funds to meet the needs of small businesses. Money-making small and midsize businesses are being turned down in record numbers, primarily because banks have become more conservative.

If successful small businesses cannot obtain funding, start-ups are even going to find it tougher. Start-ups that do obtain capital usually do so because they have collateral to back up the loan.

THE BANKING RELATIONSHIP

Despite the difficulties, entrepreneurs should not avoid dealing with banks. They shouldn't be intimidated. Bankers are businesspeople, and they are in business to make money by making loans. If they do not make loans, they will not be in business for long. But most bankers won't be attracted to far out, revolutionary concepts. They prefer the familiar, the orthodox.

All small business people are going to need a banker, whether they need funds or not. The bankers may be needed for references, credit lines, or a host of other services. Whether funding is needed at the moment or not, you should get to know your local banker. Determine which banks cater to small business; which one lends to start-ups (if any); and what the requirements might be.

Meet the banker and build a relationship. Dealing with bankers is similar to dealing with clients. To be successful, you have to listen and understand what they look for in borrowers, and ask yourself if your company (and you) meet the criteria.

Most banks favor one or two types of businesses. Some are interested in high tech, others in manufacturing, and a number have carved a niche among service providers. Once a bank begins to specialize, its loan officers learn the industry. They study cash flow, receivables, distribution, and other elements that influence the health of an enterprise. If a bank does not specialize, chances are its loan officers will know little about a particular enterprise, and they are less likely to make the loan because they do not understand the business. Find a bank and a specialist in your field, if there is one.

Shurcut never got his loan. Ultimately he borrowed the necessary capital from a relative. In fact, that's where most small business people get funds today—from friends or relatives. That's one reason many start-ups are funded initially with $10,000 or less—it is hard to generate much more from friends or relatives.

CREATIVE SMALL BUSINESS FINANCING

If the funds are not available through family or acquaintances, investors are a possibility, but with them there often are difficulties. Investors are going to ask for collateral, too. While lenders might not ask for as much collateral as the bank, the borrower is going to have to put something up. And entrepreneurs usually must give up a good percentage of the business in return for funding from private investors.

Creative financing—a term that was once associated with real estate and homebuying—can be found in the small business field. It comes in a variety of forms: Some people take second mortgages on their homes and combine that with private funding; some entrepreneurs sign over a percentage of net profits each year (before taxes) until the loan is paid down.

Private lending sources are more available today because of low interest rates and even lower returns on traditional saving vehicles, such as certificates of deposit. (Should inflation heat up, however, the funds for small business will dry up because investors can usually generate a higher, safer return by putting funds into government-backed securities.)

Those who invest in small business know it is a risk, but a successful venture can show a return of 20 to 30 percent.

One of the more innovative creative financing schemes is the "guaranteed government small business loan." It works in the following manner. Entrepreneurs approach a private lender and ask for $X, and explain that the government will "guarantee the loan principal." Here's the catch. The entrepreneurs borrow twice the amount of money needed. In other words, if they needed $1,000, they ask the lender for $2,000. The borrowers invest the extra $1,000 in a government-guaranteed bond, which has a face value of $2,000 when it matures.

Obviously, the $2,000 pays off the loan, but what about the interest? Over the loan period, the borrowers pay the interest rate that they have agreed upon with the lender, but *only* the interest. When the bond matures, the principal is paid. The loan turns out to be an interest-only, with the principal guaranteed. The arrangement is clean and safe for investors, whose funds are guaranteed. If desired the bonds can be held by a bank.

START-UP COSTS AND OVERHEAD

Just how much capital is required is determined by start-up costs and overhead. Most "failure-proof" enterprises have low start-up requirements. Chase Revel recommends that you "try to keep it that way. If you need some equipment, and you have the choice of buying new or used, look closely at the old. Why pay the premium, especially if it drains your capital, which you will find you need."

He recommends that entrepreneurs check the price differences between the old and new, and evaluate how long the old will last versus the new. If the cheaper item is going to last five years, and the new one is guaranteed for ten, it may pay to buy the lower-price item because it will leave the enterprise with more cash. If things go well, you can always replace the old item down the line, when the company is on its feet.

According to Revel:

> Many entrepreneurs disregard their capital and buy only top of the line equipment. When they open, they find themselves with all the equipment, but not enough funds left to do marketing or to reach for in the event of an unforeseen problem. Don't always buy the best. Look at your capital and evaluate things first.

Shurcut initially purchased considerably cheaper equipment that was not top of the line. The equipment could do the job, and it left Shurcut with funds for marketing.

Jerry Turner investigated used equipment for his striping business but decided against it. "I could have saved money, but in this business used equipment may mean you are just inheriting someone else's problems. Many times used striping and paving equipment can be more trouble and take more maintenance hours than they are worth," he says.

Equipment and supply costs vary with every business, but the least capital-intensive enterprise is consulting. Because Shurcut needed certain equipment and inventory as well as a storefront establishment, his business was considerably more expensive to launch than a consulting practice such as Dennis McCuistion's. It was not as costly as Turner's striping/paving business, which needed expensive, heavy-duty equipment.

CALCULATING ONGOING EXPENSES

Shurcut's case is an interesting example of how much it takes to start a business and what is involved in determining costs. "It's easy to make mistakes when you open a business for the first time," he says. "Luckily, I worked for groomers before and knew what the most expensive start-up and ongoing expenses would be."

Shurcut credits his experience with helping him avoid an almost-fatal mistake.

There is more to business than just looking at rent and lease costs, the utilities, supplies, and marketing costs. With groomers, I quickly discovered one of the most costly and frequently overlooked expenditures—especially by neophytes in the field—is electrical.

We use blowers all day long on animals, and
there are few utilities more expensive than electric.

Running blow dryers eight to 10 hours a day could
easily push an electric bill to more than $300 a month—
which was just about how much Shurcut paid in rent for
his first shop.

Mobile groomers have an edge here. Besides charging
premium prices for the convenience, they park in customers' driveways and hook into the home's power sources.
Even if customers have their pets bathed and groomed
weekly, their electric bill doesn't rise significantly. But bathing and drying as many as 25 to 30 pets a day causes
Shurcut's bill to skyrocket. Thus electricity is a significant
cost for groomers with storefronts.

MANUFACTURING MARGINS

Costs can be deceptive in other industries, too. In manufacturing, for instance, accurately determining costs can be
difficult. There are fixed expenses in numerous areas (screening bottles or buying and printing packaging, ingredients,
and so on), but product production costs rise and fall depending on orders and quantity. The higher the order, the
lower the per unit cost. Even with a hit product, manufacturers frequently make mistakes. One entrepreneur who hit
upon a hot product and sold it almost as fast as he could
product it nearly went out of business because he ignored—
or forgot about—one seemingly insignificant cost.

This manufacturer, who produced shampoo, thought
that every item had been calculated in determining the
ultimate price of the product—ingredients, bottles, caps,
overhead, cardboard shippers, and the like. But he forgot
one thing: the cost of the large carton in which the card-

board shippers were placed when multiple cases were shipped. That carton added 10 cents to the cost of each bottle, a margin that came to more than 30 percent of the manufacturer's net profit. If he had not caught the error before he sent out price lists, he'd have found himself in financial difficulties.

Manufacturers have other problems, aside from hidden overhead items. They also have a distribution problem, or the woes of dealing with a middleman. Someone has to get the product to the retailer, and that usually is the distributor. Owners of service and retail businesses are more fortunate. They do not have a middleman between them and the end user (the consumer or tradesperson). Even when manufacturers have the funds to put into the product, they still have to battle archaic distribution practices in most industries, practices that run everyone's costs higher.

For instance, if a manufacturer produced a widget for $1 (including office overhead and marketing costs), she would sell the item to a distributor for $2. (Note: To determine how much to charge distributors, manufacturers almost always double their manufacturing costs.) The distributor would price it at $3 to the retailer. The retailer would sell the widget to the consumer or end user for the suggested retail price of $6. (Of course, retailers can charge more or less than this suggested price.) The system seems simple, but complications arise for manufacturers. The figures on the following page are a simple illustration of this.

If this manufacturer sold 31,476 eight ounce bottles, then each bottle would absorb another $1 in overhead. Thus, to cover overhead and product cost, each bottle would cost the manufacturer $2.26 and it would sell to a distributor for $4.52.

Manufacturers figure their overhead, product and marketing costs, and then arrive at a suggested retail price.

One problem is that it is difficult to get products distributed. For instance, a distributor may service 150 retailers in

Manufacturing Costs
    Overhead

Rent	$500
Telephone	200
Water	18
Gas	55
Electric	250
Advertising	1,500
Taxes	100
	2,623 x 12 = $31,476

Product Costs

Bottle/container (8 oz)	.10
Cap	.03
Screening	.03
Ingredients	.55
Carton (12 bottles per)	.05
Shipping (one case)	.40
Shipping carton	.10
	1.26 (per 8 ounce bottle of product)

an area, and in each of the stores he provides 10 product lines from a dozen different manufacturers. The distributor has already worked out discounts and advertising allowances for those lines. The manufacturers have agreed to it, the store has, too, and everyone is familiar with the program.

Distributors can take on a product from a new manufacturer, but they're not fond of doing so. They have to develop a new discount structure, convince the store's purchasing agent the product is worthwhile, readjust the shelves and displays, and possibly even pull one of their existing lines because there is not enough room. Most distributors figure that they gain little by campaigning for new products.

Distributors prefer the easy way; unless a product has

lost its market, distributors seldom pioneer new ones. They wait for the store or for consumers (or customers) to ask. Only after repeated requests will retailers ask distributors for the product.

One other policy compounds these difficulties for manufacturers—they must refund 100 percent on any product that does not sell. This policy can cost manufacturers a fortune. Suppose, for instance, a distributor turns an order over to a company for 40,000 widgets. The company gears up, manufactures the product, and ships to the distributor, who ships to the retailer.

One, two, three weeks pass. One day the distributor gets a call from the store saying sold 200 widgets were sold and to come get the rest. The store receives a complete refund or, in some cases, credit on other merchandise that the distributor handles. Either way the manufacturer is stuck. She has nearly 40,000 widgets she has not been able to sell, plus she has to refund the money, and she still has to pay for the raw materials and overhead. It is not uncommon for many large chains to order huge quantities of a product and return them.

"It is no skin off their nose," says Don Kracke, who has marketed more than 100 items to firms ranging from manufacturers to retail. "Plus, if they give you the goods back and you have a difficult time staying in business, they may never have to pay you for the goods they did keep and sell. Devious? Perhaps, but some large department stores and other chains have perfected this approach. They take small, one-item manufacturers and bury them— perhaps accidentally—with this approach."

Even companies that have a hot product can run into trouble. Retailers or distributors buying only one item have no incentive to pay early. If they want a whole line from a manufacturer, they have incentive: They must pay or they will not get the rest of the line.

Motown Records, which has been one of the most successful labels in the industry, ran into difficulties with distributors and retailers shortly after it had its first hit record. Slow payers, the distributors and retailers showed no inclination to pay within 30, 60, or even 90 days.

The label was unable to collect until it came out with its second record—another hit. Every distributor wanted the record, but Motown refused, unless all bills were paid. The ploy worked, and Motown was off and running.

Distributors and retailers pressing for co-op advertising funds also strap manufacturers financially.

It is easy to see why manufacturing can be enormously costly and a high-risk venture. As Don Kracke said many times: "Manufacturing is best left to Taiwan and Korea. In this country, it has become extremely rough to try and make a living at it."

Manufacturing is no longer a haven for entrepreneurs. The risk is great and the obstacles significant, much more so than a traditional service business.

SERVICE BUSINESS COSTS

Kendall Shurcut had to figure his costs—everything from rent and utilities, to shampoo, conditioners, supplies, and dryers. His initial rundown looked like this:

Monthly Costs

Rent	$300
Shampoo	110
Taxes	60
Telephone	60
Marketing	150
Water	18
Gas	55
Electric	275
	$1,028

Shurcut's next challenge was to figure out how much to charge for each service he offered. One consideration was what competitors were charging. Another was: How much money did he want to make?

Although good groomers (or people who are good at any business) can charge a premium, they cannot go too high in a competitive field or they lose out.

Shurcut surveyed the area and found the average groomer was charging around $25.

Then Shurcut estimated how many dogs he would bathe on an average day and a heavy day, keeping in mind that heavy days were usually Fridays and Saturdays during the summer or flea season. During those three months, Shurcut estimated he would have two heavy days every week.

Total baths on the heavy days:
30 (baths) x 24 (days) = 720

Shurcut closed Sundays and Mondays. On Tuesday through Thursday he estimated he would bathe an average of 17 dogs. He would take a week off, thus he would have

52 weeks
−1 vacation
‾‾‾‾
51
−5 (total number of heavy days translated into weeks)
‾‾‾‾
46 weeks remaining x 5 days per week =   230 days
230 days x 17 baths per day   = 3,910
Plus 720 baths on heavy days   =   720
Total number of baths per year   = 4,630

That figure is the maximum and assumes Shurcut does not have down time. Realistically, he will have approximately 10 to 15 percent down time because of equipment breakdown, marketing efforts, or product shortage. Total number of baths after downtime: 3,710 baths.

Shurcut decided to up his fee slightly from that of the average groomer, to $28. That would give him a yearly gross of $103,880.

From that, he subtracted costs:

$$\$1,028 \times 12 = \$12,336$$

He had additional labor in the form of one full-time assistant and two part-timers. The full-time assistant earned $7.50 an hour and worked forty hours a week, for a total of $1,200 per month. The part-timers earned $5 an hour and worked fifteen hours a week each, for a total of $150, or $600 per month. Monthly salaries and insurance connected with them came to $2,400 per month, or a total of $28,800.

	$12,336
	+ 28,800
Total yearly expenses	$41,136
	$103,880
	–41,136
Net profit before taxes	$ 62,744

Shurcut's net was significantly higher than most groomers, and for good reason. Most groomers, when they hire assistants, usually wind up splitting the monies generated from grooming (which takes place after the animal is bathed). Kendall avoided this split and paid an hourly wage by hiring someone who had never worked in the industry but wanted to learn.

Shurcut says:

> Paying someone 45 to 55 percent commission is too much. That's why most grooming shops only net

about $20,000 per year. I was not going to work five full days a week for that kind of wage. Additionally, if you run a grooming shop and bring in a groomer as an independent contractor and split their fees, you have to make sure they pay their taxes. Otherwise, the IRS can come after you. In many cases they have driven groomers out of business with rulings that say they must pay the taxes the contractor did not pay. If the so-called independent contractor did not pay taxes, the IRS may construe them as an employee, and you can be liable for their taxes.

LOW REP OVERHEAD

Lana McKendry has a relatively low overhead in her rep business, but she also operates on a thin percentage from the manufacturers who hire her. Reps earn anywhere from 4 or 5 percent to 15 percent. It depends on how strong the manufacturer happens to be and how much resistance there is to its line. The more resistance, the tougher it is for a manufacturer to get a good rep. When it does, it has to pay more.

Commissions on McKendry's $20 million worth of sales during the past year could run anywhere from $500,000 to more than $3 million, depending on the industry and resistance. Lately McKendry has watched reps being squeezed by many of the large retailers. She says:

The rep goes in and establishes the account. Once the product starts selling well, some of the retailers will try to bypass the rep. They call the manufacturer directly and propose cutting out the rep. That way the manufacturer can save money—and, of course, the retailer wants part of the savings passed on to their company. It can be a tough business, but if you have developed a good relationship with the manufacturer, they will stick with you . . . most of the time.

McKendry's start-up and overhead costs are, of course, minimal. She can rent reasonably priced space, and many reps even work out of their homes. The main expenditure is fax and telephone, significantly less overhead than Shurcut's.

Reps have to examine product lines and potential carefully before they negotiate a percentage. Remember, the percentage can be anywhere from 2 to 15 percent, depending on the industry and other factors. That is a significant swing; however, not many product lines pay 15 percent and sell well. The lower the commission, in general the better the product moves. Reps who saddle themselves with accounts that are all paying 15 percent may believe they have an edge, but when a product does not sell, the commission is meaningless. Astute reps usually evaluate the line and forecast how much they might sell during a 12-month period.

Some reps set a goal as to gross income and a limit on the number of manufacturers they will handle. They use the "limited clientele" as a selling point when they approach manufacturers, and ask for higher commissions in order to keep their clientele small. Every manufacturer would like to have limited-clientele reps. The fewer accounts they take on, the more time they spend on each. Working for only a few manufacturers is a good selling point, but the rep must produce to keep the business.

McKendry has always produced, and despite her close industry ties to most of the buyers, her biggest problem has been with buyers trying to bypass her to get a better price. "In most businesses the thing to remember is that it is a business, and sometimes people will do anything to cut costs or make a buck. When you are out there on your own, beware," she warns.

Jerry Turner and other striping contractors run much higher overheads than reps; the major item is labor. Although the business can be started for under $10,000, there is ongoing overhead in the form of equipment, too.

"Your equipment has to be the best," Turner advises. "You cannot afford breakdowns, because that's money out of your pocket. Invest in good equipment and you will not run into that problem."

Turner never has. Thanks to his reliability, he is busy year-round and frequently travels out of state for jobs. He says:

When the economy slows, you have to realize everything else will, too. Even though striping wears out just as quick from year to year, regardless of the economy, owners will resist spending money if business is down. They'll hold off. During the early 1990s, when California was in throes of a recession, I did a great deal of work in neighboring states. My overhead, because of the travel, soared and my net profit was lower, but when you have equipment and employees, you have to keep them busy. That's one thing about a labor-intensive business like ours. You can make good money, but you always have to be looking for your next job, so you can keep your crew busy.

Determining Turner's net profit can be difficult. Although he grossed more than $2 million this past year, he earned it in a variety of parking lots. Unlike grooming, where you charge a fixed price per animal, a striper's rates vary and depend on the lot, the type of stripes required, and the number of spaces.

Stripers usually charge per space and according to what has to be done. Turner says that a straight white line could run $2.20 per line. A 50-car lot—with 100 lines—could be completed in an hour.

Special spaces mean higher rates. A handicapped, blue space with its handicapped designation may run a company $25. The amount the striper gets not only depends on the difficulty of the job, but the competition as well. In markets where there is an abundance of stripers, each cutting rates, that $25 might be a $10 job. Turner stays away from jobs where the owner is seeking huge discounts, because "You can't make money [from them]. All you do is stay busy, but there is no sense being in the business if you cannot make a dollar."

THE QUALITY FACTOR

Turner has found that offering a quality, guaranteed service where the work he does lasts longer than that of competitors is its own best selling job. "I might lose a job here or there because someone is willing to charge less but, for the most part, I won't because the owners know we do quality work that is going to last longer," he says.

Striping offers an excellent profit. A lot with about 100 spaces will generate around $1,500 and will take two to three men all day to do. Turner pays his best workers about $10 an hour. His expenses for a job breaks down as follows:

Expenses

Labor $350
Paint   150

That leaves a gross profit (before overhead and taxes) of $1,000 on a $1,500 project.

Overhead eats up about another 30 percent, for a gross

profit, before taxes, of around $700. Gross profit translates into just under 50 percent for the business, an extremely high margin for any enterprise. In fact, a good striper with one machine will gross somewhere between $200,000 and $250,000 per year, with a gross profit (before taxes) of around $80,000 to $110,000.

Turner has expanded his business to seal coating, the coating and sealing of lots. "You can seal coat an 80,000-square-foot lot in a day, and your labor and materials would be under $2,000. The job would go for anywhere from $3,500 to $4,000. There's another case of a striping-related business that is going to earn more than 30 percent after tax."

SEASONAL SWINGS AND PRICING

Turner's business—and many others—have seasonal swings. You cannot pave or stripe lots in the rain, and work is difficult in winter when the ground is frozen. Revenue and contracts diminish.

As mentioned, Shurcut's business drops in winter, too. Animals do not get as dirty as fast and fleas aren't as much of a problem, so owners don't bring their pets in as frequently. Mike Goldberg's heaviest time of the year is the spring and summer, when manufacturers want ads placed for their new flea products and foods. In winter the pet industry as a whole goes through a slower period.

Slow periods hit every industry, and the key to surviving and prospering during those times is knowing the business and when they are most likely to happen. For planning and cash flow, you must know when the slow season will occur.

Mike Goldberg's pricing has been set by industry standards, which are anywhere from 15 to 20 percent per ad. Working with seven to 10 publications and selling anywhere from 10 to 20 ads a month has enabled Goldberg to earn more than $100,000 a year. Typically, industry trade ads are expensive. They reach a specialized audience and companies pay a premium. *Groom & Board*, a publication that goes to approximately 20,000 groomers in the U.S., costs about $2,000 per page, and would generate a commission of anywhere from $300–$400.

Goldberg's ad production runs about $60,000 per month, or more than $700,000 a year. That translates into commissions of more than $100,000. Of all the "failure-proof" businesses, Goldberg's has one of the lowest overheads. Working out of his home, his telephone and fax run less than $500 per month.

BILLING TECHNIQUES

Venture Marketing Billing

Dennis McCuistion works out of his home, too, and as a consultant he can value his services in several ways: hourly, cost plus, percentages, and so on. One of the most popular fee-setting techniques is venture marketing, in which the consultant is compensated strictly on the percentage of the increased sales of a client company.

For example, take a company that grosses $2 million and is growing at a rate of 10 percent a year. It would be expected that next year's gross would be $2.2 million, or a 10 percent increase. In venture marketing, the consultant does not take a fee but can earn anywhere from 50 to 75 percent of the gross that is above the $2.2 million forecast. In other words, the consultant is given credit for the increase above $2.2 million, and he or she earns a percentage of those dollars. If the company that was expected to gross $2.2 million grosses $2.5 million, the consultant earns a percentage of the $300,000 increase.

Performance-based Approach

McCuistion has developed a variation of the percentage technique. Sometimes for his consulting services, he accepts a smaller percentage, plus a lower fee, but he never waives the complete fee. Whenever possible, he takes a piece of the company or stock through performance but, he says, "that does not happen often. You have to earn some kind of fee when you have employees and overhead. If you go for the complete crap-shoot and are compensated strictly on performance—that is, developing a solution and implementing it so the problem disappears—then you need sufficient capital behind you. Or you have a business with minimal overhead and no employees." The performance-based approach appeals to clients who have a shortage of capital.

Burn Rate Billing

Consultants can use still another technique, one that appeals to clients with some funds but not enough to pay the going rate for their services. This is called the "burn rate." It works this way. The consultant—in this case, McCuistion— estimates how long it will take him to complete a project, say, three months. He then bills the client his usual rate for three months. If the project goes beyond that time, the client pays only half McCuistion's usual fee. McCuistion absorbs the loss.

This approach appeals to some clients because they have put some time limit on the consultant's services. Consultants want to complete the project within the burn rate period—for any more time, they'll make only half their normal fee. Even though most consultants have low overhead, halving a fee can lead to a loss.

Only experienced consultants should use burn rates, for only they can accurately estimate how much time a job will take. They will *not* get burned. Inexperienced consultants, however, can wind up losing money.

Most of McCuistion's clients prefer that he quote them a fixed price. If the project lasts longer than McCuistion expected or if he puts in more time than contemplated, he absorbs the loss.

"Overhead Plus Profit" Billing

Many consultants arrive at their billing rate through an "overhead plus profit" billing system. First they determine their yearly overhead and desired profits. Then they divide this into yearly workable hours and establish hourly rates. For example, if overhead is $4,000 a month, and the consultant wants a gross profit of $8,000 per month after overhead, she must earn $12,000 per month. If she wants to take home $8,000, she must earn more because of taxes.

Once consultants determine the monthly gross income they need, they calculate what their hourly rate would be. There are approximately four working weeks in a month, or 160 hours (40 hours per week). Divide the number of working hours per month (160) into the amount of money needed ($12,000), and you get an hourly rate (here $75 per hour).

Before settling on that rate, however, consultants have to figure on several other things. Not all working time produces income. Marketing and bookkeeping time, while important, is not revenue producing. Consultants must estimate how many hours per month they will spend in non-revenue-producing activities, subtract that number from the monthly total of hours available, and then recalculate the hourly desired rate.

THE CONSULTANT COMPARISON

The advantage McCuistion (and other) consultants have in billing and dealing with clients is that comparing consultants by their fees is difficult. When a client wants McCuistion, she is willing to pay McCuistion's fee because she has heard good things about him. That is not true with other products. Consumers can go to the supermarket and compare, for instance, one brand of canned peaches with another. Some brands are more expensive than others, and they may taste better. Consumers can make a choice on the basis of price (the well-known brand may be more expensive) and be assured that if they pay more, they generally will get a better-quality product.

Consulting is entirely different. Buyers are choosing an intangible, and price seldom has anything to do with the quality of what is being purchased. There is no guarantee that Consultant X, who charges twice as much as Consultant Y, actually is better than Y.

BILLING RATE OF EMPLOYEES

Whether "failure-proof" business owners are consultants or hire employees for projects, they should calculate an "hourly multiplier" when billing and bidding every job.

If, for instance, an employee makes $15 per hour, a multiplier of approximately three should be used to cover salary, overhead, and profit. In other words, if Jerry Turner bids on a job and figures it will take two hourly workers one full day to complete it, he should use their wages as one of the criteria for the bid. If they make $120 for the day, Turner has a multiplier that will enable him to recover the $120, plus the funds it costs him to pay for their taxes, insurance, and other benefits. In other words, he cannot just collect $120 and pay his workers the $120. If he did, he would be losing money. He must calculate those costs into his bids. Some entrepreneurs double the wage rate, while others even triple it. Typically, a doubling is needed to pay employee salary, taxes, other costs, and allow for a profit. A tripling of the daily rate is usually reserved for the principal or senior manager on a project. It is always part of the bid or project estimate.

Regardless of how fees are derived, every entrepreneur in this book communicates their charges clearly to clients and prospects. Nothing is as devastating to a relationship— and nothing will drive clients away quicker—than a misunderstanding about fees.

Lana McKendry always quotes percentages clearly to prospective manufacturers, and she outlines the policy on expenses that are incurred on their behalf. She has a written agreement, too.

Mike Goldberg makes it clear from the beginning that he expects his publishing clients to pay for mailings that he makes on their behalf, and what his standard commission will be (usually 15 percent). All his agreements are in writing.

Kendall Shurcut lets his clients know that bathing a dog who is in good condition will cost $X, but bathing one that has not been taken care of will cost $XX.

Bob Levinson provides a menu of prices and services to all clients and a simple, one-page letter of agreement that states his terms and conditions. Jerry Turner always has a letter of understanding, as does Dennis McCuistion.

Jay Horoki has a written contract, spelling out terms and conditions and detailing his cleaning procedures.

Whenever possible, small business people "put it in writing." Doing so clears up any misunderstandings from the beginning and avoids problems later.

FIVE-POINT FEE CHECKLIST

All of the "failure-proof" business owners adhere to the following five-point checklist when it comes to fees:

1. Communicate the obvious. Do not assume the client knows anything about the job you are going to do or what it takes to get it done.

2. Explain everything if the client seems to have questions about the fee. Even if a point seems simple and mundane, be sure to explain it carefully. Remember, the client does not know the intricacies of the business, whether it is grooming, consulting, repping, or janitorial work.

3. Never say the job will be easy. This frequently leads the client to believe that the fee should be lower.

4. Display confidence in your ability to do the job. Clients hire outsiders because they believe these people are experienced and know what they are doing.

5. If there is some doubt or question about your ability, cite some other similar jobs you have done.

Shurcut explains the bathing process and how it differs from grooming—and why it takes so long. Dennis McCuistion is careful to stress the experience that is needed for some jobs. Jay Horoki explains how difficult it is to clean certain parts of an office and why some of it is so time-consuming. Lana McKendry carefully outlines the amount of work she has to put in when it comes to making sure her client's (manufacturers) displays are properly placed.

MARKET-AVERAGE CHECKLIST

All successful businesspeople discussed also have carefully evaluated their markets, rates, and what they should be charging. Most of the techniques for doing so fall into this 12-point market-average checklist.

1. Call competitors to determine hourly and daily rates.
2. Make enough calls to get an accurate cross-section. Make sure you are calling those within similar marketing (or market) areas.
3. Determine where you want to be on the rate scale— high, low, or in the middle.
4. Break the rates into hourly fees.
5. Multiply the hourly rate by the number of workable hours in a month.
6. Subtract a percentage of workable hours for activities other than the work performed. Remember, there is marketing and bookkeeping involved.
7. Subtract these hours from the total hours you can work. Get a new hourly base.
8. Determine your potential monthly gross with this method.
9. Determine your monthly overhead. Don't forget the "small" things, such as telephone, water, and electric. These items mount up. The typical overhead:
   a. rent
   b. utilities
   c. cleaning service (if you are renting and it's not included)
   d. telephone

e. postage

f. equipment rental/leases

g. insurance/worker's compensation

h. auto costs, if company paying for it

i. letterhead/stationery

j. secretary/other employees

k. taxes (social security, disability, etc.)

10. Determine the profit (before taxes) you want to make.

11. Does the monthly gross allow for the profit you are after? If not, readjust your salary, cut overhead, or look at your fee structure again.

12. Make sure you do these things before you open the enterprise. An accurate cost, billing, and desired profitability schedule are a must in every business.

In the next chapter we will look at what happens once these "failure-proof" entrepreneurs determined their costs, devised billing systems, and raised the capital needed to open their doors. We will take a closer look at the unique marketing techniques many utilized in order to turn a mundane, everyday business into an enterprise that was virtually "failure-proof."

7

How They Marketed and Built Their Businesses

There's an adage in the promotion business that says "You can't hype a stiff." In other words, if people do not want your product or service, no amount of advertising or promotion is going to convince them otherwise.

One of the best examples of the futility of trying to market a product or service that people dislike took place a number of years ago. A record company in England was marketing an extremely successful European group, and on several occasions it had tried to introduce the act to the United States. On each occasion, it was futile. American companies took the group's recorded products, released them with complete promotional programs behind each one, but the outcome was always the same—failure.

Over 18 months, U.S. companies released a total of six records by this group, and each flopped. Finally the British company turned to its leading American subsidiary and insisted that it not only release the next record but promote it as well. Reluctantly the U.S. company agreed, budgeted funds, and started to make elaborate plans for the debut of record number 7.

What happened was astounding. The U.S. company hired a special promotion force that visited radio stations across the country in an effort to sell them on this "new" group. A few stations decided to give the group a chance and played the record.

From the day it first aired, the record was an instant hit. Consumers deluged stations with requests for it and flooded record stores buying copies. Within 30 days almost half the radio stations in the country were playing the song, and demand continued to build. It was as if no one had even remembered those first seven flops.

A promotion executive working for the American label called one of the best-known, highest-rated television shows in the country, told them about the group and how hot the record was in England, and described the initial acceptance it had in the United States. The show's producer, always looking for an act with appeal, decided to give the group a chance. He booked it for one appearance.

Thus, in February 1964, the Beatles made their initial appearance on the *Ed Sullivan Show*, where they sang their seventh U.S. release (and the first one to become a hit), "I Want to Hold Your Hand." And the rest, of course, is history. (Interestingly, every one of the six records that had bombed in the 18 previous months was rereleased and became a hit as well.)

The Beatles are the perfect example of the inability of a company to "hype a stiff." During 1962 and early 1963, despite intense promotion by record companies in the United States, the Beatles were unable to sell any product. Even when their 1962–early 1963 product managed to get some air time, it did not sell. Yet by the end of 1963, "I Want to Hold Your Hand" was in demand by virtually every station in the country.

What happened? What made the difference? First, consumer attitudes in the United States changed radically between early and late 1963. Attitudes do change. Take the baby boomers, for instance. At one point they were buying BMWs and spending time in France. Now they are raising families and watching television.

The Beatles' U.S. release of "I Want to Hold Your Hand" was just over a month after the assassination of President John F. Kennedy. (The actual release date was December 26, 1963.) People were looking for something light and uplifting. The British foursome was it.

Capitol Records, the company that introduced the group in December of 1963, budgeted $50,000 for the national campaign but the record soared up the best-seller charts even before much of the money was spent. Why? Timing. Now people wanted the record.

All the marketing expertise in the world cannot sell a product that customers do not want, need, or accept. But once there is a predisposition for the product, watch out. If it is promoted, it will seldom miss.

THREE MARKETING QUESTIONS

Before any marketing campaign is undertaken, the businessperson should ask some basic questions:

1. Where is my market?
2. Who are my customers?
3. How do I reach them?

The record label knew the exact answers to those questions, and so do successful, "failure-proof" business owners. Take, for instance, Dennis McCuistion. He knows his market is bankers and/or financial executives who reside throughout the country. They are primarily in one industry—banking.

One marketing technique that McCuistion developed to reach his potential clients was giving speeches. In about 100 speaking engagements each year, he reaches 10,000 to 20,000 financial executives. McCuistion's topic usually is strategic planning for banks and small businesses. He says:

> I was in California giving an address to bankers at their lending conference. One of the people who heard me said he was going to have a board retreat and hired me to do a session with the board. Then he referred me to another bank board. I met the directors of that second board, who said they had problems with management, and they hired me as a consultant.

In the consulting field, there are few marketing forums

more potent than the speaker's podium. When a consultant has been asked to give an address, he or she is considered an authority, an expert.

Before McCuistion gives any speeches, he makes sure that those three marketing questions are answered. Why? McCuistion does not want to waste his time speaking before a group of insurance executives. They are not the people who will hire him. Thus, asking where your market is and how to reach them is the critical first step. In McCuistion's case bankers were his market, and he could reach them by speaking at various (banking) industry seminars and conventions.

In Tony Walton's case, the market could be as nearby as the closest office complex, and he can reach them by simply knocking on doors. For Jerry Turner, it is simply a matter of picking a commercial area that has parking lots and, as Walton would do, knocking on doors.

At times, in their anxiety to get the doors to their business opened, entrepreneurs can overlook these questions. But all "failure-proof" business owners carefully target their audience by knowing where the market is, who the customers are, and how they can be reached.

Every retailer or those entrepreneurs with a storefront location (e.g., Kendall Shurcut) can confidently say that their market is local, within about two miles. A two-mile radius is about the limit someone will travel to visit a retail establishment, unless the goods are unusual. Most customers are local.

Who are the customers? In Shurcut's case, they are dog owners. Other retailers should be able to answer this question just as easily. Determining how to reach the customers is the most difficult part of the three-part equation. Advertising is not always the answer. In many cases it is not affordable, and none of the "failure-proof" businesses in this book utilized it to draw or build a customer base. "Failure-proof" business owners do not rely on advertising

bypass the middleman and retailer and go directly to the end user.

Fluster thought his idea was great, but he had little capital to manufacture and promote the item and generate distribution. Therefore he decided to produce and distribute it himself. He solved part of his manufacturing problem by approaching a plastics company and proposing that it make a prototype. If it was successful, he would use that company to manufacture the product. The company constructed the prototype, and Fluster came up with a way to research and market the product at the same time.

HOW TO GET FREE ADVERTISING

He went to a local college and told the public relations' instructor he was willing to pay a student $50 to write a new product news release. The instructor supplied the student, and Fluster's next move was to photograph the "ketch-all" while it was being used. He paid a photographer $50 for the shot, took it to a duplicating house, and had 100 copies made.

Fluster's next step was to find the publications that would be interested in running the release—magazines that would reach his market. The obvious market was the restaurant trade. Virtually every restaurant in the country might be a potential customer because the device would save labor and food. Fluster visited the library, looked up *Bacon's Magazine Directory* and photocopied the section entitled "restaurant." *Bacon's* is a complete directory that lists the name, address, and telephone number of thousands of trade publications. It divides them into categories—restaurants, automotive, data processing, and so on. Fluster picked the 26 listings in the restaurant field.

He also went to the "general magazine" section of *Bacon's* and found several hundred publications that printed new product news releases. Among them were *Better Homes & Gardens* and *Good Housekeeping.* He copied down their telephone numbers, and, for the next three days, he called each publication, asking the name of the person who handled news of new products. He carefully packaged the news releases the student had put together along with the photographs, and addressed them by name to the new product editors of each of the publications. Then he waited.

A week later he began making calls, asking the editors if they received his release and if they had had a chance to read it. Did they have any questions? As a result of his perseverance, *Nation's Restaurant News*, the largest trade publication in the industry, ran the item along with the photograph. Three major consumer magazines, including *Good Housekeeping* and *Better Homes & Garden*, also ran it, although not until three months later because of deadlines.

Two days after the item ran in the restaurant publication, Fluster received a call from one of the largest food brokers in the country, asking if the ketch-all could be customized. That is, could Fluster put the broker's logo and name on each one, and what would the price be in quantities of 100,000?

Fluster worked out the customization, arranged financing through the plastics manufacturer once a purchase order had been cut, and within 90 days was in the manufacturing business. That first year he did more than $250,000 in volume through orders for the ketch-all. His total promotion investment was less than $300, for the photos, news release, duplication, and mailing.

IMPACT OF PUBLICITY

Fluster did what many entrepreneurs have mastered—using news releases and/or promotional techniques to test market and market products at a low cost. Positive publicity not only opens the door to sales and inquiries, but it has credibility, too. Despite the pessimistic attitude many consumers have toward the media today, we still tend to believe what we see, hear, and read.

Regardless of the size of the area, marketing does not have to be expensive. In fact, money does not guarantee customers, and none of the "failure-proof" enterprises was launched with a huge expenditure. A host of simple, inexpensive, easy-to-implement marketing approaches are available. Virtually every one will quickly let entrepreneurs know if they have a hit or a "stiff." Publicity is one, and Al Fluster utilized it. So did Lana McKendry and most of the "failure-proof" business owners.

When McKendry opened her rep firm, she relied on a news release to the trades (1) to let every purchasing agent/buyer know she was in business and, equally as important, (2) to get the word out to manufacturers—through their trade publications—that a new rep firm had opened, one with experience in the home center industry. She sent her release to purchasing journals (publications delivered exclusively to those in the purchasing field) and to trade magazines that were serviced to manufacturers.

Kendall Shurcut used a release, too. His was targeted at the numerous local suburban newspapers that run items about new businesses in the area. Those publications reached his audience, the consumers who lived within a few miles of his storefront. Editors of most local publications are cooperative, because they know if the business grows and prospers, it may one day become an advertiser.

McCuistion targeted several audiences with news releases. His first target was the banking trade, where there were many publications that his colleagues read. He also wrote an opening announcement release for management and business-oriented magazines, which reached executives who needed help in dealing with bankers.

Bob Levinson sent his opening announcement release

to the local chamber of commerce newsletter and local suburban daily newspaper. As a Rotary member, he was able to place an announcement in the local Rotary newsletter, too.

Jay Horoki sent a release to a local trade journal that was delivered to commercial landlords and other property owners.

Even Ginny Anderson, the mobile groomer, used a press release to announce her "grooming on wheels" enterprise and the fact it would provide service at a consumer's door. It was a relatively new concept, and two of the local suburban newspapers ran her release.

In general, before sending a news release, the successful entrepreneur asks where are my customer(s), and what publications do they read? When those two questions are answered, the businessperson knows where to send the release.

The media can be a potent, free publicity tool for every business. Chase Revel remembers the lift that the media gave *Entrepreneur*. While the magazine was still in its infancy, the *Los Angeles Times* saw a news release on the company, investigated it further, and decided to do a lengthy business piece on Revel, extolling his ability as an entrepreneur and his talent for picking up on new businesses and small business trends before anyone else in the country. The highly complimentary piece made an immediate impact on the firm's business, but Revel took it a step farther. He received permission for a small fee to reprint the piece and use it in a mailing to customers.

Each month Revel mailed more than 1 million catalogs, which were filled with mail order offers and discounts for consumers who purchased one of his start-up manuals. Typically, he did well with the mailing, averaging a 1.5 percent return and an $18 to $20 order. Then he had the *L.A. Times* story reprinted on the back cover of the next catalog. The results, says Revel, amazed him. The return jumped to nearly 2.5 percent, and the average order increased to more than $30. "It's the credibility of the media," he theorizes. "A *60 Minutes* report can make or break a business, and a positive story in a major publication can have an enormous impact, as well."

UTILIZING THE MEDIA

Most marketers and astute small business owners are aware of the power of the media, and they use it. Often companies run special sections in print (newspaper/magazines)—"advertorials." These editorial/advertising productions are purposely made to look like editorials. Why? Credibility. Even the "advertisement" line on top of the advertorial fails to hinder its impact. A well-written advertorial will outpull and outsell an ad of the same size.

That fact has not been lost on marketers when it comes to television. "Infomercials," commercials dressed up to look like real shows, are on every channel. In the past they seldom ran on network affiliates or during prime time, but the battle for commercial dollars has become so intense that now you can find infomercials airing every day of the week at any time and on every station.

While McCuistion has not done an advertorial, he is a frequent guest on local television news shows, talking about the economy and the banking industry. Television producers, however, do not just call anyone (unless it's the president or some other well-known figure). Businesspeople have to let producers and/or shows know they are available and that they are experts in a specific area. McCuistion indicates his availability with a note every two to three months. Usually it refers to some current news event and ties McCuistion into it. If the producer is planning to run something on the topic, McCuistion may be contacted because he is local and knowledgeable. Shortly after the government had passed a new tax bill, McCuistion sent this note to a public service show that tackled economic issues.

> Dear (producer's name)
>
> With the new tax act becoming law, banking—as well as a number of other businesses—are going to be impacted in our community. At the same time, consumers throughout our area are going to be effected as well. For example, parts of the tax act will make it more difficult for some companies to expand. Thus, unemployment could go up.
>
> As a consultant who has spent the past 25 years in the banking industry, I would be happy to guest on your show and comment on the bill and the changes it may bring to our city.

This note led to a guest appearance on one of the city's leading television news shows. Needless to say, it also enhanced McCuistion's image as an authority in the industry.

"Failure-proof" business owners have utilized the power of the media to help them in other ways. For instance, financial consultants frequently put together public service–type brochures with such titles as "How to Avoid Investment Pitfalls" or the "10 Most Common Mistakes Made When Investing."

Bob Levinson put one together: "The Ins and Outs of Small Business Advertising—How to Save Money." Kendall Shurcut did a simple, four-page brochure entitled "Taking Care of Your Animal in Flea Season." He treated the brochure like any he might offer: He wrote a new product release about it and sent it to the local media.

Because these businesspeople are not obviously selling anything through these brochures—rather they are helping consumers avoid mistakes—many media people regard them as public service brochures and run the release. Should consumers write for a copy of the brochure, the businessperson has generated a prospect—because most people don't ask for brochures and/or information on a subject unless they are potential customers.

For instance, the brochure seekers—in this case would-be investors, people who are interested in running small business ads for their company, or owners of flea-infested pets—want answers to their questions. The brochures give businesspeople the opportunity to dispense advice—and plug their enterprise at the same time.

This form of marketing takes place on all levels. Sometimes syndicated small business columnists list "free" offers for brochures and other advice at the end of their column. As long as the brochure seems to be assisting the public and not trying to sell them something, editors let it run. The names generated are usually prospects.

MEDIA ASSISTANCE

News releases that have public service–type offerings tend to be printed and used by media more than other types. Once again, *Entrepreneur* is an example of how one company used the media for maximum marketing assistance. Editors at the company put together a 48-page booklet entitled "Business Opportunity Frauds." The publication covered the most common business opportunity frauds and gave consumers advice on how to avoid them.

The booklet, along with a news release, was sent to more than 200 business editors. The company then hired a clipping service for three months to monitor the number of publications that ran the release and the value of the space. More than $60,000 worth of free advertising was generated, and nearly 55,000 people wrote to the address listed in the story for a free copy of the manual. All they had to do was include 50 cents for postage and handling. While *Entrepreneur* lost money on the mailing, it generated nearly 55,000 names of potential buyers of one of the company's manuals. Thus the booklet and release were lead generators.

Not every release is going to be printed, but some entrepreneurs have found other, equally effective ways of utilizing the media in order to market their products and services. For example, several business owners run "columns" in the local suburban or metropolitan newspapers. They pay for the space and construct their "ad" as if it were an editorial.

"Free" offers can be made through these columns, too. For instance, Levinson ran a column and at the end offered his brochure on "small business advertising" to any businessperson who wrote to him. He generated 35 requests from the local suburban newspaper, and four eventually became accounts.

This phenomena is happening in all professions. Veterinarians, financial consultants, and even pet groomers run columns. In Kendall Shurcut's case his column discusses "grooming problems" and how to avoid them. It also talks about the effect different shampoos have on animals and when the best time is to bathe dogs.

WRITING THE RELEASE AND FINDING MEDIA

The major benefit of all this publicity, whether it is paid-for advertorials, news releases, or stories written about an entrepreneur's products or services, is the reprint value. That is, once it appears businessowners cut it out, paste it up, and use it as a mailing piece to present and prospective customers. It carries credibility and weight with prospective customers, and it can increase business significantly, much as it did in the case of *Entrepreneur*.

To be effective, news releases have to be written and targeted correctly. Penning a release does not require creative writing talent. Releases consist of five elements:

1. Who
2. What
3. When
4. Where
5. Why

Just the facts, and those facts should be found in the first paragraph. Don't include adjectives and superlatives in a release. Many small business people who feel uncomfortable with the writing process have, like Al Fluster, gone to local colleges and recruited journalism students to construct the releases for them.

Targeting the correct media is more common sense than anything. Local media lists can be generated through chamber of commerce offices. More extensive lists can be put together through *Bacon's Magazine Directory* and *Bacon's Newspaper Directory*, which list every trade and consumer publication imaginable. Many libraries carry them. If not, Bacon's is headquartered in Chicago.

Successful placement of a release depends on one other thing—whether the release is written with the audience in mind. Consumer publications will not print a release that touts a special new weather-resistant parking lot paint that Turner's company is utilizing. General consumers will not be interested, but owners and purchasing managers of numerous chain and department stores (the people who hire Turner), will be. These executives are reached through trade, not consumer, publications.

Information on Kendall Shurcut's opening an all-natural grooming shop that specializes in grooming dogs with nonpoisonous products is geared to local consumers. Hence the local suburban newspaper should receive the release. If sent to a major metropolitan daily, however, chances are that the release will never run. Metro papers cover huge areas, and Shurcut's shop caters to only one small segment (and area) of the market. Metro papers won't run it because it does not apply to all their customers.

Mike Goldberg sent his release on his rep service for magazine publishers to advertising trades as well as to publications that reach magazine publishers. It is not consumer news. Even though he caters to the pet industry, publications in that area would not be interested in running it because they cater to pet owners, not the publishers of magazines in the industry. "Failure-proof" business owners who utilize releases always look at the ultimate audience before they send one out.

They also try to develop and maintain a relationship with the media. As mentioned, in McCuistion's case, media relationships were critical. After he developed them, reporters called him and asked him what he thought of a new banking regulation or other changes that might impact the industry. The more they called and quoted him, the greater the authority he became in the eyes of his prospective customers.

McCuistion did something that many service and/or consultants do. He had a small Rolodex card made with a tab that said "Banking," so it would be filed under "B" in someone's Rolodex. The card listed his name, telephone number, and some facts about him—25 years experience in the banking industry. Knowledgeable in the area of regulation, new laws, banking problems, and forecasting the industry."

He sent out dozens of cards, along with a note to both consumer and trade reporters. The note simply said "If you need any assistance in putting together banking stories, especially those referring to new regulations, give me a call." Reporters never know when they might be assigned a story, and good resources are difficult to find. They save and file Rolodex cards, and McCuistion's became a mainstay to a half-dozen key banking writers.

Other successful entrepreneurs practice similar techniques. Although they might not send Rolodex cards to the media, they do send them to prospective and current customers. The tab on Shurcut's card reads "Dog Grooming." Tony Walton had one made that said "Computer Repair."

McCuistion and Levinson also send notes at the end of every third quarter to reporters. The message pertains to the fact they are involved in banking and small business/ advertising and aware of some of the current and future trends in the industry. The reason—by the start of the third quarter, most publications and writers are beginning to look at year-end stories and trend pieces for the coming year. A timely note led to editorial coverage for more than one entrepreneur.

GENERATING CLIENTS VIA TALKS

McCuistion is not the only speaker among the "failure-proof" entrepreneurs. There is opportunity in virtually every industry. Shurcut speaks at pet shows and groomer exhibitions; Goldberg lectures at advertising seminars during trade shows; McKendry offers advice at marketing sessions that are held for manufacturers; and Levinson talks at local chamber meetings in which small business people are given advertising and marketing advice.

McCuistion takes the talks a step farther. He generates additional exposure by capsulizing his speech in a news release and sending the release out a day ahead of the talk. When he puts contemporary issues in the speech (how new legislation or regulations may impact the industry and consumers, for example), the media usually runs portions of it.

The emphasis on media coverage and exposure is not accidental. Entrepreneurs are increasingly looking to marketing approaches other than advertising because of expense. Advertising does not necessarily generate customers for these "failure-proof" enterprises. Bankers call McCuistion because of his reputation and some of the things they have read about him. Shurcut's clientele come from word-of-mouth. McKendry's and Goldberg's clients come from personal contact.

"Speaking and writing articles are excellent ways to generate leads," says McCuistion. "I don't know many cases where advertising has generated any clients for a consultant." Although they are in different fields, Turner, McKendry, Goldberg, Shurcut, Levinson, and others agree.

What makes an impact is developing mailing lists and then communicating with prospects via the mail, newsletters, and brochures. "A brochure," says Goldberg, "does not land the account but it portrays an image of your company. It pays to spend money on a brochure. If you deal on the telephone as I do, the first impression a prospect is going to get is visual—your brochure. Make it look good, and you are ahead of the game."

Turner says the brochure depends on the business and client. "The purchasing people and managers I see don't care about brochures. They want results and prices. Most of my business is dependent upon the job I did last time. A brochure can impact a consultant's business, but in mine it is primarily relationships and past performance."

McKendry agrees. "It's a relationship business. What counts more is who you know and the communication you have with them."

Shurcut communicates frequently. He sends cards to owners on their pet's birthday and cuts out articles from pet magazines relating to animal care and sends them along with a note to clients. "People may not read everything I send, but it shows them that I care. If you're in a business like this one, that's important."

McKendry sees buyers at trade shows and she calls manufacturing clients at least weekly. She says:

> Buyers do not want you dropping by to say hello. They're too busy. When I see one it is after I have made an appointment, and it always relates to a product I have—or want to—put in the home center. I never waste their time. Never waste anyone's time. If you do, they begin to think all your calls and notes are unimportant. Every contact should have a purpose. Socializing can be left for dinners following trade shows.

Goldberg speaks to his publishing clients at least once a week. Prospective advertisers are on his mailing list, and they usually get correspondence from him on a monthly basis.

> I don't push advertisers. In today's market, that's a mistake. I try to supply my prospects with information and material they can use. For instance, I might send a dog food manufacturer a note about a special nutritional issue we have coming up. Or I might tell them about a survey that we recently completed relating to dog foods. It's more of an educational/information process. The more they know, the more likely they are to become a client (advertiser).

COMMUNICATION—MARKETING TOOL

If there is one definitive statement that can be made about these business owners, it is that they all believe in communicating frequently with clients (and prospects). Each, however has a different way of doing it, and none pressures clients for more business.

Newsletters are a tool, as well. Levinson uses a quarterly that he puts together and sends to clients and prospects. It contains advice and small business advertising tips, and runs four pages. Ginny Anderson has a one-page monthly that goes to dog owners and covers nutritional and health issues for animals. She gets most of the input from manufacturers, who provide her with additional brochures that can be sent to customers.

Direct Mail—Generating Leads

By offering free information, brochures, and other material, businesspeople generate leads. Shurcut gets brochures from shampoo manufacturers on animal care, and he sends them to clients along with a note. McKendry has developed a 10-step display approach that enables home centers to show and sell goods more effectively. Buyers ask her for the information sheet, and she takes a supply to hand out at shows. At the bottom of the sheet is an 800 number, plus a tear-off form that can be mailed to her company for "additional tips on displaying and marketing product." The tip sheet is a subtle way of providing service and making sales inroads when it comes to buyers. The same sheet can be used with manufacturers, who are always interested not only in getting their products in-store but in getting them displayed properly.

Jay Horoki uses direct mail to landlords and tenants. He offers free janitorial analysis of facilities to show tenants/landlords how technology can help them save them money on cleaning. Horoki's technology is a computer program he worked out. He goes through the office/building with the prospect, takes notes, and feeds information into a laptop computer. Within minutes he has a printout showing prospects how long it should take to clean the facility and how much they should be paying. It's impressive for prospects to view, and although Horoki may not get every account, it leaves an impression in their mind that his company knows what it is doing.

Even if businesspeople can't afford to put together brochures and newsletters, they can tap into distributors, manufacturers, and suppliers. They all usually have classy, well-put-together material that a business owner can supply to clients—usually for free. By offering free information, brochures, and other material, businesspeople generate leads.

PROMOTIONAL IMPACT

Promotions are a mainstay. Delia Ornaz uses Val Pak, a direct mail coupon service that delivers to as many—or as few—doors as she desires. Inside, there is a $10-off coupon plus a complete description of what Ornaz's service does and a cost rundown. There is also a brief paragraph about her "walkthrough" and the fact she will redo anything found to be unsatisfactory. One other thing she includes that few of her competitors think about—testimonials from clients.

Although he no longer has to do it, Shurcut used to work promotions with nearby pet stores where he would give "free dog baths" on a particular day. The pet shop usually had a shampoo manufacturer donate the shampoo, and Shurcut gave his time. The store advertised the event and benefited because it always drew traffic. Shurcut benefited, too, since it gave him a way to meet prospects.

Promotions where both parties benefit are ideal. McCuistion frequently worked with banks that were interested in building a better image among consumers. He would volunteer a weekend afternoon or weeknight evening to provide financial advice to consumers on behalf of the bank. It helped the bank build its local reputation, and McCuistion had an account when the bank needed outside services.

This give-and-take goes on in every small business. In many cases it has helped turn new, struggling enterprises into thriving ones. Promotions need not be elaborate, and they are almost always inexpensive, another characteristic of those that are utilized by "failure-proof" small businesses. Perhaps one that best illustrates the value and the impact of a well-constructed promotion took place in Los Angeles.

A businessman had opened a small hamburger stand on a streetcorner not far from downtown Los Angeles. He had used virtually all of his capital for rental, food, and grand-opening banners and was left with only a few dollars for marketing. The man started to think of different ways in which he could promote his enterprise. He looked at his market and asked the key questions: (1) Where is my market? (2) Who are my customers? (3) How do I reach them?

Hamburger stands draw from a small market. They are local and few people will travel more than a mile or two. The prime customers for fast food are kids. Now, what technique could he use to reach them?

It took some brainstorming, but the owner came up with an idea. He went to the local high school, sat down with the principal, and proposed several things. He told the principal that he was a local businessperson who cared about the community and the kids in it. He would like to work with the school to develop a program that would help recognize and reward youngsters who had gone "above and beyond." He wanted the principal and faculty to pick five kids each week and give him the names. They could be the best scholars or best athletes, it did not matter. He just wanted the names, which he would place in a small space ad that would run every Friday in the high school newspaper. The named youngsters could tear out the ad and bring it to his hamburger stand, with identification, for a free hamburger, french fries, and soda.

The principal liked the idea and so did the teachers. It was a way to recognize students in a constructive manner. The following week, five names were picked. As the promotion rolled into its second month, the owner began to notice that his stand was drawing the high school students away from competing hamburger stands. Within six months no other stand could compete with him, and within a year he catered to more than 90 percent of the students in the school.

Less than 10 years later, he was a millionaire, and eventually his one stand grew into a chain of more than a dozen. Even today, years after that initial promotion, no one can compete with his locations. He is still involved with local schools, but his program has been greatly expanded. Today, at many campuses, he donates money for football, baseball, and basketball uniforms. Or he gives funds to the student body for events.

Interestingly, even today, he does little consumer advertising. Once a week he might place a small, one-column ad in the *Los Angeles Times'* sports section. Most of his advertising and promotion is still geared for the high schools—his prime market.

What was it about the promotion that generated so much business? Status. Students who were recognized achieved higher status because their names were in print. Other students envied them. That status carried over to the hamburger stand. Students gained status not only from having their names in the papers; being seen at "Tommy's" was even cooler.

IMPACT OF RECOGNITION

Recognition proved to be the difference in this campaign. Few consumers are immune from it. Everyone loves to see their name in print and to be recognized. Stroke someone's ego, and you are on the road to building a new customer. Small businesses can do that. They can also utilize the same technique that Tommy's developed to build their own customer base.

Many people believe that developing and marketing a small business is difficult, because most of these enterprises are small, generate limited revenue, are faced with expensive media costs, and usually have a shortage of capital.

But marketing is not an obstacle. Every one of the "failure-proof" enterprises in this book was created and marketed products and services with little capital. Many were creative and used innovative, inexpensive techniques—techniques that not only worked, but enabled them to build "failure-proof" businesses despite the fact that competition for the customer's dollar is now at an all-time high.

While each is an amazing success story, even more important is the fact that the techniques used by these small business people can be used in many other businesses today.

Appendixes

Appendix A
News Releases

News releases can be of significant help to small business people in search of free advertising space. The following releases were composed by owners of "failure-proof" businesses, and they all led to positive media exposure in addition to generating leads.

Release #1: Consultant Opens Business

News Release
For Immediate Release

For Further Information
(Tel. #) (Your name)

McCuistion Opens
Bank Consulting Practice

Dallas, Tex. Sept. 5—Dennis McCuistion, a 25-year veteran of the banking industry, has opened McCuistion & Associates, a consulting firm specializing in the banking and finance industry.

McCuistion, who was formerly (title) of (name of institution), will specialize in handling regulatory problems and in assisting banks and savings and loan institutions with new federal requirements.

In making the announcement, McCuistion said "as everyone knows, we have just gone through a period of extensive reorganization in the industry, and with the new regulation and requirements, banks and s&ls are going to have to provide much more information and analysis than they did in the past. Our firm was set up specifically to aid the institutions in adhering to the many new government regulations and reporting requirements."

McCuistion's office will be located at (address). His telephone number is (number). A native of (home state and city), McCuistion attended (name of college), where he majored in (subject) and specialized in the banking industry.

Release #2: Seminar Conducted
by Small Business Person

News Release
For Immediate Release

For Further Information
(Tel. #) (Your name)

Seminar to Cover New
Banking Regulations

(City), (Date you mail)—"The New Banking Regulations and How They Will Impact Banks and S&Ls in (name of city)" is the title of a free, two-hour seminar that will be held Monday, Feb. 19, at the Dallas Marriott, from 4 until 6 P.M.

The session, which will cover the Jan. 15 regulations that were just implemented, will be hosted by Dennis McCuistion, a 25-year-veteran of the industry and a specialist in regulatory matters.

During the session, McCuistion will cover new reporting requirements, reserve changes and how they will impact banking institutions. In addition to McCuistion, Jack Allred of the Federal Depository will also be on hand to discuss the changing regulations and answer questions.

Seating is limited, and those planning to attend are asked to RSVP to McCuistion's office (tel. number).

Release #3: Free Brochure Designed to Generate Leads

News Release
For Immediate Release   For Further Information
        (tel. #) (Your name)
Free Brochure Details
How to Prolong Parking Lot Pavement

(City), (Date you mail)—"How to Maintain and Prevent Parking Lot Deterioration" is the title of a free new brochure being offered to lot owners and operators by Turner Construction, a (name of city) paving and striping firm that specializes in lot maintenance and paving.

The brochure contains more than two dozen hints on how owners can prolong the life of the surfacing and striping in a parking lot, and can be obtained by either calling Turner (tel. #) or sending a request to (address).

Turner Construction has been in the maintenance/striping business for more than 10 years, and has resurfaced more than (number) of lots in the area during the past year.

Release #4: Opening of New Business Release

News Release
For Immediate Release   For Further Information
                                 (tel. #) (Your name)

McKendry Opens Rep Firm

(City), (Date you mail)—Lana McKendry, a five-year-vet-
eran of the home center industry, has opened McKendry &
Associates, Inc., a manufacturer's rep firm, which will handle
placement and display of hard goods in retail centers.

Ms. McKendry, who was formerly with Home Depot,
will concentrate on lines that are produced by manufacturers in the 11 western states, including California, Washing-
ton and Oregon.

The firm, which is located in Orange County, California, will be headed by Ms. McKendry. Vice president is
(name), who also spent the past five years in the home
center industry. Telephone number for the new company is
(number).

Release #5: Opening of New Business Release

News Release
For Immediate Release

For Further Information
(tel. #) (Your name)

Goldberg Opens Agency

(City), (date you mail)—Michael Goldberg, a veteran advertising salesman and marketing specialist, has opened his own advertising sales firm, which will specialize in representing publishers in the pet industry field.

Goldberg, who spent the past five years as an advertising salesman for (name of company), will represent noncompeting publications from pet industry publishers. His first account is (name of magazine), a pet industry publication that is aimed at the industry's retailers.

Goldberg will headquarter in New York at (address). His telephone number is (tel. #).

Release #6: Release on Free Brochure

News Release
For Immediate Release

For Further Information
(tel. #)   (Your name)

Cutting Liability, Worker's
Comp Rates Subject of Restaurant Brochure

(City), (Date you mail)—"How to Prevent Workmen's Comp and Liability from Rising" is the title of a new brochure being offered at no cost by Vicky's Valet Company to restauranteurs throughout (name of city).

The brochure, which details six factors that cause workmen's compensation rates to rise and six others that impact liability, also outlines how restaurant owners can eliminate those factors. It can be obtained by either calling (telephone #) or writing (address) Vicky's, a valet service that has been located in (name of city) for the past (years).

Release #4: Release Pertaining to Speech

News Release
For Immediate Release

For Further Information
(tel. #)   (Your name)

Need for Marketing Approach
On Part of Small Businesses

(City), (Date you mail)—In a speech before more than 100 (name of city) businesspeople at the chamber of commerce weekly luncheon, Bob Levinson, president, Levinson Advertising & Public Relations, urged "every small business person to develop an organized, effective marketing plan" if they intend to survive in today's competitive environment.

Levinson, who has been in the small business advertising field for more than a decade, went on to say that the greatest "danger to profitability and survival that small businesspeople face is their inability to adequately develop a marketing approach that will help them reach both present and past customers."

Levinson went on to cite government statistics, which showed that more than 70 percent of all business failures in (name of city) during the past five years "were directly attributable to a lack of marketing."

Levinson also addressed the question of budgeting and how much a small businessperson should allocate for yearly marketing. He also detailed an approach that would enable every businessperson to "design their own low-cost advertising and promotion program." The approach—which his firm turned into a free brochure, is available from Levinson's office, located at (address and telephone number).

Release #8: Release Pertaining to Promotion

News Release
For Immediate Release

For Further Information
(tel. #) (Your name)

Johnson Named VP
of McKendry Associates

(City), (Date you mail)—John Johnson has been named vice president, McKendry Associates, the national rep firm that specializes in handling display and placement of manufacturer's goods in home centers. The announcement was made by Lana McKendry, president of the (age)-old company.

In his new position, Mr. Johnson will be responsible for sales and marketing activities in an 11-state region. He will also coordinate McKendry's marketing efforts, with a dozen field representatives in those states.

Mr. Johnson comes to McKendry Associates following 11 years with (previous company), where he was vice president in charge of sales. Prior to that he was with (name of company), where he was purchasing agent.

Mr. Johnson will headquarter at McKendry's corporate offices in (name of area). He will report directly to Ms. McKendry.

Release #9: Release Pertaining to Community Involvement

News Release
For Immediate Release

For Further Information
(tel. #) (Your name)

Janitorial Firm to
Co-Sponsor Food Drive

(City), (Date you mail)—Jay Horoki's Janitorial Service, Company, Inc., will co-sponsor the annual (name of area) food service drive for the hungry and will supply (quantity) of canned (type) goods, while its employees collect additional donations from companies throughout the area.

The canned goods will all go to (name of organization), the group that specializes in feeding hungry from the (name of area).

As part of the co-sponsorship, Horoki will give each volunteer employee a half day off with pay in order to participate and collect the canned goods. Horoki's firm is (years) old and provides services to major industrial and commercial centers in the (area or city).

Appendix B
Direct Mail Checklist

When constructing a direct mail letter to generate an appointment or interest, the "failure-proof" businessperson always keeps the following checklist in mind.

1. Have a good, strong opening line to grab the reader's attention.

2. Have a USP (unique selling proposition) within the letter. USPs are what make your company different from your competitors. In the case of Kendall Shurcut, it is the fact he does not use poisons, but he still does the job. With Jay Horoki, it is his computerized checklist to ensure that clients always get *their* cleaning needs handled. A USP sets your company apart.

3. Have a beginning, middle, and end. Do not ramble. Think letters through. Good letters are like entertaining stories. They keep the reader's interest and satisfy them.

4. Do not hard sell or twist arms.

5. Supply readers with information that they can utilize, something that will relate to their needs.

6. Be sure to explain any point that might be confusing. Don't use slang or acronyms.

7. Conclude with a call to action. That is, get them to make a call (to you) or state when you will call them.

Appendix C

Client Letters/ Correspondence

Send this note to a present or previous customer regarding an item that you saw in the newspaper.

Note #1

Dear

Thought you might enjoy seeing a copy of the article that ran on your company in the (date) issue of (name of publication).

It was a fascinating piece and certainly says a great many good things about your company.

Congratulations.

Sincerely,

Jay Horoki

Send this note to a client or prospect.

Note #2

Dear

Congratulations on the promotion!
    I just read about it in the (name of publication), and judging by the comments, it is certainly well deserved.
    Once again, congratulations and all the best in the new position.

Sincerely,

Bob Levinson

Send this type of note to a prospective client following a meeting.

Note #3

Dear

Just a short note to express my appreciation for the time you took in discussing your company and the services we might be able to provide.

Your firm is certainly fascinating and has enormous potential. I look forward to the future and working with you and your staff.

Once again, many thanks for your time and interest.

Sincerely,

Dennis McCuistion

Send this note to a potential client following an initial meeting.

Note #4

Dear

Both (name) and I enjoyed meeting your staff and hearing firsthand about the (name) project. Unquestionably, it is going to be a winner.

We are in the process of putting together a proposal that I think you will find quite interesting. It should be in your hands within the next week.

I look forward to discussing the project with you in the near future.

Sincerely,

Lana McKendry

Send this note to someone after a referral.

Note #5

Dear

My sincere thanks for the reference and helping to set up the meeting with Mr. Brown. He was quite interested in our capabilities, and I was fascinated with his company. It's a great firm with tremendous potential.

I'll let you know how things develop. Once again, my thanks for setting it up.

Sincerely,

Jerry Turner

Send this note to a client after you complete a job.

Note #6

Dear

Just a short note to express my appreciation for utilizing our company the other evening to handle the (name of party) wedding and reception.

We are grateful for the opportunity, and hope we can do it again. Once again, many thanks.

Best

Vicky

Index